PRAISE FOR *GOOD TO BE GRAND*

"When you start to read this book, be prepared to smile, learn, think, reflect, reminisce, and chuckle . . . all the way to the end. Armed with current knowledge on baby care and child development, you will be ready to enjoy and enrich your family life in the role of a grandparent."

—LOIS KERCHER, PhD, RN, *past president of American Organization of Nurse Executives*

"Many of my patients prepare for having a baby by reading up on the topic, but *Good to Be Grand* is specifically for grandparents and offers a wealth of important information most grandparents probably don't know. I wholeheartedly recommend Cheryl Harbour's book to couples looking for an excellent resource to pass on to their own parents in preparation for grandparenthood."

—LISA MAZZULLO, MD, OB/GYN, *coauthor of* Before Your Pregnancy: A 90-Day Guide for Couples on How to Prepare for a Healthy Conception

"Cheryl Harbour's *Good to Be Grand* is a great read for any new grandparent. I recommend the book as a resource for parents and grandparents alike. Harbour's organization around 'What's Still True?'/'What's New?' gives grandparents and new parents a chance to open a dialogue about generational differences in parenting while exploring together what is best for the newest member(s) of the family. *Good to Be Grand* is solidly grounded in current knowledge of child and family development yet accessible to anyone interested in learning more about the life-changing experience of grandparenting, which I believe to be potentially the most important family role of this century."

"Becoming a grandparent is full of blessings as well as often unexpected challenges. In this engaging book, Cheryl Harbour shows us that grandparenting isn't just a simple reboot of the parenting role, but will require learning new skills, both communicative and practical, as well as rediscovering forgotten joys. She is a wise and appealing companion for this journey and she has written a lively, accessible, and informative guide that will be welcomed by anyone embarking on this wondrous phase of life."

"If only every stage of life had a book like this to go with it! *Good to Be Grand* not only informs but highlights the opportunity to approach grandparenting with intention and along the way discover new areas of personal growth."

GOOD TO BE GRAND

GOOD TO BE GRAND

Making the Most of Your
GRANDCHILD'S FIRST YEAR

CHERYL HARBOUR

Foreword by
HILLARY RODHAM CLINTON

BenBella Books, Inc.
Dallas, Texas

BenBella Books, Inc.
10300 N. Central Expressway, Suite #530
Dallas, TX 75231
www.benbellabooks.com
Send feedback to feedback@benbellabooks.com

Printed in the United States of America
10 9 8 7 6 5 4 3 2 1

Library of Congress Cataloging-in-Publication Data
Names: Harbour, Cheryl, author.
Title: Good to be grand : making the most of your grandchild's first year /
    Cheryl Harbour ; foreword by Hillary Rodham Clinton.
Description: Dallas, Texas : BenBella Books, Inc., [2016] | Includes
    bibliographical references and index.
Identifiers: LCCN 2015036663| ISBN 9781942952329 (hardcover : alk. paper) |
    ISBN 9781942952336 (electronic)
Subjects: LCSH: Grandparenting. | Grandparent and child.
Classification: LCC HQ759.9 .H3645 2016 | DDC 306.874/5—dc23 LC record available at http://lccn.
loc.gov/2015036663

Editing by Vy Tran
Copyediting by Stacia Seaman
Proofreading by Kimberly Broderick and Jenny
    Bridges
Text design and composition by Aaron Edmiston
Front cover design and interior illustrations by
    Connie Gabbert
Full cover design by Sarah Dombrowsky

Printed by Versa Press
Photo on page x by Jon Davidson, Office of
    President Clinton
Photo on page xiv by Jennifer Jacobson
Photo on page 104 by
    AmericanPhotographic.com
Photo on page 108 by Jim Nolte

Distributed by Perseus Distribution: www.perseusdistribution.com
To place orders through Perseus Distribution:
Tel: (800) 343-4499
Fax: (800) 351-5073
E-mail: orderentry@perseusbooks.com

**Significant discounts for bulk sales are available. Please contact
Aida Herrera at aida@benbellabooks.com.**

To Jackson, who opened my eyes to new possibilities,
and to his parents, Raleigh and Brooke-Sidney,
who made Jackson possible.
To Bob, Todd, and Ryan—who paved the way.

In memory of Jean Acton, the grandest grandmother.

CONTENTS

FOREWORD

I cannot stop grinning. I have that "grandmother glow."

My friends had told me there is no greater joy than being a grandparent. Of course they're right. I know that now.

I know the boundless love, awe, and gratitude that filled my heart when I held Charlotte for the first time. And I know that being a grandparent is different than being a parent.

When my good friend Cheryl Harbour asked me to write this foreword for *Good to Be Grand*, just after Charlotte's arrival, I couldn't say no. Cheryl and I shared our childhood in Park Ridge, Illinois. We've also marked life's great milestones together, from graduations to marriages to the births of our children—and now Cheryl and I both celebrate the greatest blessing: grandparenthood. As newly minted grandmothers, we proudly trade photos and swap stories about our brilliant infant grandchildren. It's often said that children don't come with instructions. Well, neither do grandparents. When Bill and I found out that Chelsea and Marc were expecting a little one, we wanted to learn all we could and understand our new roles. We were looking for information and inspiration. *Good to Be Grand* is a blend of both.

This book is not meant to replace a scientific journal or in-depth research on child development—you may want to dig deeper and become an expert in all areas on your own—but it is a good place to start. It reminds us of those basics of child care that remain as true today as they were when Bill and I raised Chelsea. But it is also a concise compendium of up-to-date thinking and practices, including some insights into both popular trends and emerging science that may save us from wondering and worrying.

For example, new brain research is underscoring just how important the first five years of life are for later development. In a baby's growing brain, seven hundred new neural connections are forming every second, laying the foundation for learning, behavior, health—all the things children need to grow up to be productive adults. We now know that loving adults play a critical role in this development, because when we talk, read, and sing from the moment a baby is born, we are helping those neural connections form and literally helping to build the baby's brain.

Early exposure to talking, reading, and singing also helps build a baby's vocabulary, setting him or her up for a lifetime of success. But for struggling parents who might work multiple jobs or have to keep odd hours, reading, singing, and even finding time to talk to their children can be difficult. As a result, research tells us that by age four, children in low-income families hear about thirty million fewer words than their more affluent peers, and therefore know many fewer words by the time they start kindergarten. Experts call this the "word gap," and it puts children born with the fewest advantages even further behind.

Talking, reading, and singing with a child every day are some of the best things we can do to help that child have success in school and beyond. The good news is that you don't have to be a parent to make that impact. You could be a neighbor, a pediatrician, a pastor, or a child care provider. You could be a grandparent.

Through your grandchild—as this book shows—you become part of a web of relationships. It does take a village to raise a child. Whether you have a large or small family, a close-knit community or extended network, all of us have a special role to play in shaping a child's life.

For Bill and me, being grandparents has been transformational. I have found my singing voice again. When Chelsea was eighteen months old, she reached her little finger up, put it on my mouth, and said, "No sing, Mommy. No sing." But Charlotte doesn't seem to mind.

Bill takes Charlotte by the bookcase, making note of books she should read when she gets older. I know he looks forward to the day he can discuss Maya Angelou's *I Know Why the Caged Bird Sings* or Ralph Ellison's *The Invisible Man* with her.

I know we are neither the first nor the last people to feel that sense of transformation and inspiration in being grandparents. After all, new life gives you fresh perspective. It makes you want to be the very best grandparent you can be.

As Bill and I held Charlotte for the first time, we looked at her with wonder and excitement. We can't wait to watch her learn and grow as we embark on the journey of grandparenthood together.

I hope you enjoy reading this book by my friend Cheryl and that it is a good companion for your own journey.

—HILLARY RODHAM CLINTON

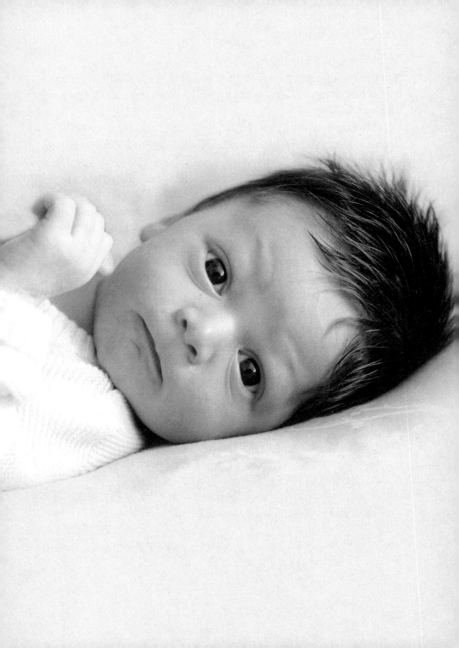

INTRODUCTION

For most of you, at least twenty years or so pass between when you become a parent and when you become a grandparent. Not only do we forget things during those years, many things also change. New medical procedures are discovered, the science of child development advances, and parenting theories transform.

When I was about to become a grandmother for the first time, my oldest son (the father-to-be) was thirty-seven and my youngest was twenty-five. That means two and a half decades had passed since I was accustomed to balancing a baby on my hip. I asked my friends who were already grandparents what I'd need to learn in preparation. They responded eagerly, but most of them interpreted my question as an expression of some kind of insecurity about my new role.

"Don't worry," they said.

"You'll be great."

"All you need to do is love the baby."

Yes, I thought, I know I can do it. And I know I'll love him. But where is the user's manual for what I'm about to share with my new grandchild? How can I prepare myself to become the very best grandparent I can be?

The parenting books I found weren't what I needed. They are too long and too detailed. They contain too much information, most of which is irrelevant for the role grandparents play. And even with all that information, what's missing is they don't explore the unique relationship between a grandparent and their grandchild.

We're the grandparents—*they* are the parents

The reason why those parenting books aren't right for us is that what's essential for parents isn't the same as what's useful for grandparents. The most important difference of all is that, as grandparents, we are not in the driver's seat. We're in the sidecar. We're not the ones losing sleep. We're not feeling the heavy responsibility of nurturing human life for the next couple of decades. But we *are* coming along for the adventure. As grandparents, we are a valuable resource when the driver needs to take a nap, or go to the bathroom, or take a vacation, or go back to work—and then we need to be competent and calm in our new role.

Here are some examples of the practical differences:

- The parents choose the baby's doctor.
  The grandparents need to know how to reach the doctor.
- The parents decide if a baby boy will have a circumcision.
  The grandparents need to know how to care for an infant who has been recently circumcised.
- The parents will choose a car seat.
  The grandparents need to know how it works.

- The parents will develop a plan for introducing the baby to solid foods.
  The grandparents need to know what they've decided in order to prepare for a grandchild's visit.
- The parents will formulate a parenting philosophy.
  The grandparents will do their best to understand—and comply with—those expectations.

The importance of the baby's first year

As I reflect on the first year of my grandchild's life, I'm amazed at how much I've learned about the differences between being a parent and being a grandparent. As a mother, I love my three boys wholeheartedly. They are my sources of extraordinary pleasure and pride. But the grandmother experience is quite different.

I was fortunate that, as a young mother, I didn't experience post-partum depression. I was happy and ready to be a mother. I was also lucky to have parents and an older sister who provided generous support and encouragement. Even so, there were times when I was tired, confused, distracted, conflicted, and spread too thin. These are perfectly normal aspects of first-time motherhood. I rarely ran out of patience, but I certainly ran out of time.

With my first son, I adapted to the new responsibilities of parenting and made adjustments that sometimes made me feel like I was sacrificing aspects of my life that I valued. I stepped out of the corporate world (and onto the "mommy track"), but I continued with consulting and freelance writing. Still, there were times when I was about to run out the door to a meeting, dressed in my best black business suit, and the baby would spit up on my shoulder. Or he'd get croup in the middle of the night—and it always seemed to be when my husband was out of town and I had deadlines approaching. And, of course, there was the constant search for a good babysitter. I adored that first baby, but boy, did he change my life!

By the time my second and third were born, I was a much more experienced and relaxed mother. I had already learned so much of what I needed to know from that first baby—and, really, from his first year of life.

While I learned that from personal experience, science now confirms the profound importance of a child's first year. An infant undergoes amazing physical development during that year, and the connections formed in the child's brain have a lifelong impact. I am so excited to be a part of that—again! As my grandson and I progressed through his first year of life, I encountered an unexpected and equally profound blessing: the opportunity to make it one of the best years of *my* life, too.

From good to grand

Not only are grandparents in a different stage of life than young parents, they are one step removed from the newborn. The responsibilities, expectations, and demands are so different. As a grandparent, you remember the fears, anxieties, and self-questioning (along with happiness and amazement) that came with being a parent. Standing over your sleeping baby several times a night to reassure yourself with the sweet, soft sound of breaths going in, going out. Wondering if that extra crankiness at dinnertime was masking an ear infection. Having your toddler cry when the babysitter arrived so you could go out to dinner—and going out to dinner anyway. You remember those

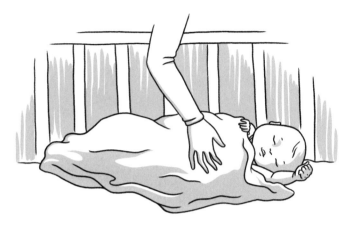

feelings, but you don't feel them the same way now because it's the parents' job to feel them. Compared to parenting, the pleasure of being a grandparent is unfettered. You can give yourself over to the moment and just enjoy. Grandparenthood is more than a not-so-instant replay of parenthood. It's not just a chance to revisit and revise but a unique journey—interesting and challenging and rewarding, all at once.

At the same time, grandparents have told me that the birth of their grandchild makes the future *personal* for them. Instead of looking down the road to make sure our children have a good life and live in a manageable world, we now need to extend that care and concern further into the unknown. We have "skin in the game" to try to preserve or improve a world in which our grandchildren will live long after we are around to help them with life. So we make the most of the time we have, beginning with the moment they're born.

As I set out to become a grandmother, I kept four goals in mind:

1. To learn everything I could to be the best grandmother I could be
2. To be a source of support for my son and his wife
3. To be a significant positive influence in my grandchild's life
4. To have fun with my new grandchild

In short, not just to have a good experience, but to make it *grand*, in every sense of the word.

This book follows the major developments in your grandchild's first year of life, from gestation and birth onward. Each chapter provides facts about what has changed about child care in recent generations, what has remained the same since our days of parenthood, and what grandparents can do to make the most of their time with their grandchildren.

CHAPTER 1

Anticipation

WHAT'S STILL TRUE

Let's face it. A new baby is a commonplace occurrence. Babies are born every day to people in every type of society, whether primitive or advanced. It happens to people who are ready to be parents and, sadly, to some people who aren't. No one has to have a license, a permit, or certification to be a parent.

But you must earn the right to be a grandparent. Unless you inherit a grown-up through marriage or adopt one late in life, you need to have raised at least one child, survived the ups and downs that go along with parenting, and maintained a connection with that child who is now old enough to have his or her own baby.

Grandparenthood happens at a stage of life when you may feel you are just about as smart as you're ever going to be. You've learned lessons about life, made mistakes, had some success, recovered from disappointments, and come to know who you basically are. All of those are great accomplishments.

Think you've seen it all? Think again. There's still a lot to be experienced if you're willing. No matter what you've done, where you've traveled, or how you've figured everything out—prepare to be bowled over by your new grandchild.

I write this with some certainty because I've heard the same thing from all directions. The CEO of one of the largest advertising agencies in the world . . . she says there's nothing that compares to being a new grandmother. An entrepreneur who wasn't around that much when his own boys were growing up . . . he now works his schedule around babysitting. A big, tough guy who never shows his feelings . . . he had tears in his eyes when he saw his son hold *his* son for the first time—and again when his daughter had her first child. Some people don't know what all the fuss is about—all the story swapping and the photo sharing—until they have a grandchild of their own.

Still, there may be a mix of emotions at first. Surprise, if you didn't know your son or daughter and their partner were trying to get pregnant, and relief, if you knew they were. Joy . . . excitement . . . a little apprehension—yes, those, too. These emotions may be stronger than you expected, but don't worry—they're perfectly normal. Regardless of your initial emotions, becoming a grandparent *feels* important. It can even feel monumental. It marks the passing of the parenting baton from you to your child.

What will it mean to your son or daughter's life? A boatload of financial and other kinds of responsibilities? The end of carefree, footloose freedom? A sign that he or she has the maturity to bring a new life into this world? Hopefully.

And what will it mean to *your* life? It doesn't have to mean "drop what you're doing" or "lose sight of everything else." It doesn't require trading in your "DREAMR71" vanity plate for "GRAMPS" or "GRAMMY." (But don't be surprised if it crosses your mind.) The experts I talked to generally agree that the best thing you can do is maintain the good things in your own life, keep what's important to you, don't make assumptions about anything, and be open to everything. What could be better at this time of life?

If you're reading this book, you probably already know you're going to be a grandparent—either for the first time or again. Maybe your son or daughter just popped the news. Maybe he or she went to extravagantly clever lengths to surprise you. Whatever way it occurred, this is beginning of all the decisions your daughter or son and their partner will make and to which you will respond. Think positively.

The point is, now you know and the fun begins. While you anticipate, you can learn and prepare. Keep reading.

Countdown to a birthday

No one has been able to alter the reality that it takes approximately nine months to have a baby. In the past few decades, pregnancy itself certainly hasn't gotten any easier.

It's still true that pregnant women often experience morning sickness—and sometimes it doesn't end in the morning but rather lasts all day. The first trimester is generally considered to be the most common time for nausea, but with some women the nausea continues throughout the pregnancy. And some other women don't experience morning sickness at all.

Experts generally agree that morning sickness has something to do with hormonal changes in the pregnant woman. The obstetrician involved in your daughter or daughter-in-law's care will probably offer advice such as getting abundant rest, eating smaller meals more frequently, taking in smaller amounts of fluid more often, and avoiding "triggers." Odors often are considered to be triggers, so be careful what kinds of meals you serve the mother-to-be.

Depending on when your daughter or son and their partner decide to announce their news, you'll have some time to prepare, too. And grandparents-to-be can definitely begin offering help and support to expectant parents.

Grandparenting is an opportunity to be renamed

It's still true that grandmothers and grandfathers often have special names, sometimes chosen according to ethnic customs, sometimes by family traditions, and sometimes grandparents even get to choose their own. Would you like your grandchild to call you Nana, Grammy, GiGi, or Ona? Gramps, Nonno, Pappy, or PopPop?

Some other common names for grandparents include:

GRANDMOTHERS

Amma, Baba, Bobka, Bubbe, Ga-Ga, Gamma, Golly, Gram, Grams, Grandma, Grandmama, Grandmere, Lolly, Mamey, Mimi, Mimsy, Nahnee, Nanny, Ne-Ma, Noni, Nonna, Oma, and Yama

GRANDFATHERS

Boompa, Boppa, Bubba, Bumpa, G-Daddy. Gampy, Grampapa, Grandad, Grandaddy, Grandpere, Grandpop, Gumpa, Opa, Papa, Papí, Poppo, Poppy, Pops, Umpa, Wampa, and Zayde

And grandchildren might come up with their very own names for you . . . something like YumYum or Grumpy. But what can you do?

Choosing a name for yourself can present a few landmines. One wise grandmother I talked to said she happened to choose the same name as her daughter-in-law's mother—so she quickly chose another. That was a contest she wished to avoid.

Names for the baby also can be tricky. Some families have long lineages of Juniors, Trips, and Treys, with ancestors to be honored. With most babies being given a first name and a middle name, some parents try to keep everyone happy. If the parents decide to name their baby after your father or your partner's father, be honored. If not, that's fine, too. In our case, my husband and I had fathers named Oliver Wilfred and Irving Celestin—and these days those seem like really big handles for little babies. Otherwise, we might have suggested our grandson be named Irving Oliver Celestin Wilfred Harbour. Alas, his parents chose something else. We remember our fathers with affection, but their names have been retired for now.

It's likely that your son or daughter and their partner are well aware of favorite family names. But think of the math. Your new grandchild may have four grandparents (or more), eight great-grandparents, sixteen great-great-grandparents, and so on. You might be invited to make a suggestion, but ultimately, the baby's name is a decision for the parents, and somehow they will make a good one.

While you wait, you might wonder

There's so much to wonder about. Will the baby be a boy or girl? Will the parents find out ahead of time or wait until the birth? How is the baby growing inside the womb, month by month? Babies still develop at the same pace and in the same ways, and if you are curious about the size and developing characteristics of the baby-to-be, you may enjoy comparing the average-sized fetus to something more tangible, such as fruits and vegetables. One side benefit of following this progression is that your empathy for the mommy-to-be will grow as the comparison begins to include a rutabaga, a pineapple, and even a pumpkin! On the opposite page is one example progression chart, based on information from http://www.babycenter.com /slideshow-baby-size.

WHAT'S NEW

In general, people are waiting longer to be grandparents because their children are waiting longer to have babies. Partially this trend results from women taking on more involved roles in work outside the home and delaying pregnancies until the time is right for their careers. Also, financial circumstances play a role. In the United States, between 2007 and 2012, at the worst of the recession, the fertility rate fell to an all-time low. The only age group that didn't show a decrease was women thirty-five and older—and they were probably aware of the biological clock ticking.

For some grandparents, this may mean taking on this new role at a later age and watching some of their friends enjoy grandparent experiences before they do. As with almost every- thing else related to being a grandparent, not putting pressure on your children is a wise course to follow.

WEEK 4
poppy seed

WEEK 5
sesame seed

WEEK 6
lentil

WEEK 7
blueberry

WEEK 8
kidney bean

WEEK 9
grape

WEEK 10
kumquat

WEEK 11
fig

WEEK 12
lime

WEEK 13
peapod

WEEK 14
lemon

WEEK 15
apple

WEEK 16
avocado

WEEK 17
turnip

WEEK 18
bell pepper

WEEK 19
heirloom tomato

WEEK 20
banana

WEEK 21
carrot

WEEK 22
spaghetti squash

WEEK 23
mango

WEEK 24
ear of corn

WEEK 25
rutabaga

WEEK 26
scallion

WEEK 27
head of cauliflower

WEEK 28
eggplant

WEEK 29
butternut squash

WEEK 30
large cabbage

WEEK 31
coconut

WEEK 32
jicama

WEEK 33
pineapple

WEEK 34
cantaloupe

WEEK 35
honeydew melon

WEEK 36
head of lettuce

WEEK 37
bunch of swiss
chard

WEEK 38
leek

WEEK 39
mini watermelon

WEEK 40
small pumpkin

Genes haven't changed, but the science has

You probably remember something about dominant genes and recessive genes from your high school biology class. That won't be enough to let you predict what your grandbaby will look like. So much new information has been discovered about human DNA. Human beings have 46 chromosomes and an estimated 60,000 to 100,000 genes. Your grandbaby will receive 23 chromosomes from each parent. So if you are really proficient at math, you will already know that number of genes could produce 64,000,000,000,000 different combinations.

Most traits are polygenic, which means multiple genes affect different physical traits. A child's environment can also influence some characteristics—such as height, weight, and personality.

We grew up knowing that brown eyes were dominant over blue eyes, but even two brown-eyed people can have a blue-eyed child because they each might contribute a recessive blue-eyed gene—or their combined amount of melanin (the substance responsible for pigmentation) could result in lighter eyes.

In hair color, dark hair is dominant over light hair, but the genetic outcome of a light-haired person and a dark-haired person is often a blend—a hair color somewhere in between. Once again, that's because individuals have varying degrees of melanin. Similarly, the skin color of a baby born to parents of two different races frequently turns out to be a blend.

Other dominant traits—which still don't guarantee any particular outcome—are dimples, curly hair, and freckles.

Geneticists continue to explore the interesting possibilities contained in our genes. For example, there are genes that cause a person to seek thrills or be able to sing beautifully or have a talent for creativity. In most cases, you can wonder, but you won't know for sure until life unfolds.

You might get a peek before the baby is born

Thirty years ago, having an ultrasound during pregnancy was an unusual event, usually taken in case the doctor wanted to have a closer look at the fetus. And the image that resulted was a grainy black and white.

Gone are those days. Ultrasounds are now three-dimensional and display a much clearer picture of a fetus inside the womb. As the months progress, facial features can be seen. You might imagine that the baby has Uncle Gerald's nose—although I confess after seeing a number of different ultrasounds, they typically look pretty much the same. Still, they are exciting to see.

Some parents have keepsake images or even DVDs made at elective ultrasound imaging boutiques. But the FDA and many medical experts discourage additional ultrasounds, except for medical reasons. The procedure is safe and uses a non-ionizing form of radiation. But it does have some effect on the body. Ultrasound waves can heat tissue slightly, and in some cases also produce small pockets of gas in body fluids or tissues. What long-term consequences this may have, for a mother or a fetus, is not known.

While you wait, you might worry a little, too

The good news is that medical advances have taken some of the guesswork and anxiety out of pregnancy, and many new tests can certainly put both parents' and grandparents' minds at ease. The parents' OB/GYN will determine what genetic tests are necessary for your daughter or daughter-in-law. Blood tests now screen for genetic disorders very accurately. Under certain circumstances—for example, if the mother is older or there is a family history of genetic problems—additional testing will be recommended. If additional testing is necessary, amniocentesis and chorionic villus sampling (CVS) are still the tried-and-true methods.

Hopefully, you can keep your worries in check and not let them spoil your anticipation. My daughter-in-law needed to have her appendix removed when she was six months pregnant. It turns out an appendectomy is the most common reason for a pregnant woman to have surgery (about 1 in 1,500), but it isn't something you'd wish for. I admit I appealed to every divine power I could think of—and kept a photo of the baby's medical ultrasound in my wallet, so I could send him positive thoughts. And everything turned out fine.

You'll need these immunizations

You definitely don't want the first thing you give your grandchild to be an illness, so make sure to have these immunizations before you meet your new grandchild face-to-face. Check the chart on the next page.

Measles, Mumps, Rubella (MMR vaccine)	If you were born in 1957 or later and aren't sure if you were ever immunized, you can get a blood test to confirm your immunity.
Influenza (Flu)	Yearly flu shot is recommended
Chickenpox	Talk to your doctor if you've never had chickenpox
Tetanus, diphtheria, and pertussis (whooping cough)	Get a DTAP or TDAP
Hepatitis B	If you're sixty or older with diabetes or work in health care
Shingles	If you're sixty or older
Pneumonia	If you're sixty-five or older

While you wait, shopping can be fun

Baby products are now big—very big—business, and you may be amazed at the variety of new toys and equipment available for today's parents. Here are some grand first gifts for new parents and babies:

- bassinet
- crib
- glider chair or rocker
- car seat–stroller combination
- baby monitor
- the Boppy (C-shaped pillow for nursing mothers)
- bouncer chair
- play mat with overarching toys
- white noise machine

- baby carrier or sling
- diaper bag (with plenty of compartments)
- Halo SleepSack
- e-reader (for new parents on those nights when everything must be quiet and dark)
- savings account or the beginning of a college fund
- weekly house cleaning (especially during the first months)
- gift cards for stores like Target and Babies "R" Us
- professional photo shoot
- keepsake jewelry engraved with the baby's name or initials

If you have a particular gift in mind, be sure to do a little research into its safety ratings, because a lot has changed since we were parents. For example, the Consumer Product Safety Commission, the Food and Drug Administration, and the American Academy of Pediatrics warn parents *not* to use a baby sleep positioner. Online retailers and parenting forums provide a wealth of information and safety ratings for various baby products. You can find safety guides for baby and child products online at http://www.cpsc.gov/en/Safety-Education/Safety-Guides/Kids-and-Babies/. And you can search for recalled baby products in this user-friendly search engine from BabyCenter.com: http://www.babycenter.com/product-recall-finder.

WHAT YOU CAN DO

Imagine yourself in your new role. What kind of grandparent will you be?

Will you be hands-on or will you stay on the sidelines? Will you love this child long distance or be up close and personal? Will a little grandparenting go a long way or will you never be able to get enough? Will you be the big, soft lap kind of grandparent, always ready to listen, a shoulder to cry on? Will you be a "memorable moments" grandparent, with tickets to Disney World or Broadway?

The truth is, you will be your own unique brand of grandparent—a blend of who you are now and who you will become throughout your relationship with this unique child. You are in the perfect position to influence this child's life. You can share not only your wisdom and experience but also the things you love—whether it's reading, dancing, fishing, performing magic tricks, bird watching, sculpting, singing, baking, or filling in a crossword puzzle.

Child development experts now know that the very earliest stages of a child's life set the course for intellectual and emotional capacity. And you can be one more very important person providing stimulation, learning, and love.

You will enrich your grandchild's life because you are who you are. And because, together, you are about to embark on a great adventure.

What do we bring from our past?

We all bring to this experience some impressions, lessons, and memories of our own grandparents, so while you anticipate the birth of your new grandchild, you might want to reflect on what kinds of role models you had.

I had only one grandmother—no living grandfathers—and what I remember most are her long red fingernails and her

big dining room table with its fancy lace tablecloth. She was my father's mother, and her husband died when my dad was only four years old. I also remember that Gram let her cocker spaniel, Buffer, sit on a chair at the dining room table on his birthday. Now that I've spent time in California, where dogs are often allowed to wait patiently while their owners dine in restaurants, this doesn't seem so odd. But back then, it was worth mentioning to my friends. It upped the ante on "do you believe what my grandmother did?"

My mother's Aunt Mabel, whom we called Baba, lived with us for most of my childhood. My mother's mother died when my mom was only nine years old, so Baba had stepped in to help her brother raise his little girl. Although not technically my grandmother, Baba did her best. A member of the Church of Christ, Scientist, she would sit by our beds when we were ill and tell us that we were God's perfect creatures and no illness could befall us.

One time my sister's toddler almost "befell" Baba. We were celebrating some occasion at my sister's split-level house, which had six steps leading from the main floor down to the family room and six steps leading up to the bedrooms. Baba, a diminutive woman in her late seventies, was about to come upstairs from the family room when little Kevin, a healthy and hale two-and-a-half-year-old, launched himself in full flight from the top of the stairs. Remarkably, Baba grabbed the railing with one hand and Kevin with the other and managed to hang on and stay standing.

That changed my view of little ol' Baba. She had strength we didn't know she had.

On one side, I had a grandmother who had pretty much been pampered her entire life. She loved us very much—but reserved that love for Sundays from precisely 1 to 4 p.m.—when she and her brother, Uncle Lester, would come to our house for dinner. During those three hours each week, she had quite enough of me and my sister, thank you very much. On the other side was a grandmother-substitute who was involved in our daily lives but who stood on the sidelines so as not to assert her own wishes in any way. Baba was so so sweet, unassuming, and self-sacrificing that she was always the quietest person in the room.

My own parents emerged from these backgrounds as active and involved grandparents. They were available endlessly for babysitting. They had regular "overnights" as their grandchildren grew older. They took their young grandchildren on short vacations. They developed traditions and favorite routines. Did they ever get tired of reading *The Little Engine That Could* and making Saturday morning visits to the firehouse? If so, we never knew it.

The wait for your grandchild will be a good time to reflect on how you were parented as well as what your parenting experience was with your own children. Many of us were raised at a time when women and men had prescribed roles. Fathers typically worked long hours outside the house, and mothers primarily were responsible for home and kids. Dad was often the disciplinarian—with the louder, sterner voice—and Mom would say, "Wait until your father gets home." (Then she'd sneak into your bedroom later to make sure you weren't too sad.) But society evolves. Today we have more working mothers (in the U.S., women make up more than half of the workforce), more stay-at-home dads, more blended families, more single parents, more same-sex parents. Within that shifting structure, families and individuals evolve, too. When we were parenting our children, we chose to either continue or change our previous family dynamics. And now, as grandparents, we have the opportunity to reinvent our style again.

As teachers of "mindful parenting," which is covered later in this book, will tell us, sometimes the old patterns of parenting we've experienced tend to inject themselves into our current lives. They may come from old wounds or ways in our past and may not be what's best for a new situation. By being aware of these patterns, however, we can move past them into a way of grandparenting that gives us more choices.

Each new grandparent brings past impressions to his or her new role—but we're not bound by them. We cook up our own relationship from scratch. The key ingredients will be: your health and physical condition, your available time, your proximity, your relationship with the baby's parents, and, most of all, your own desire and initiative.

Why do we love to be grandparents?

Not many of the things that come with age make us overjoyed. Yes, yes, there is wisdom, and no one can deny that is a good thing. There can also be a more comfortable sense of self, a rediscovery of pleasures and pastimes shelved in younger years, an exploration of new interests, a more seasoned relationship with spouses and others in the family, a relaxation of old expectations. Come to think of it, a lot of positives come with age. Yet most of us don't run toward the signs or symbols that designate us as older (except maybe senior rates at cinemas and airlines). But we gladly adopt the label of grandmother or grandfather. We can't wait to tell the world. We don't care if people do the math and figure out how old that makes us. As a grandmother I know once said, "Being a grandparent is the sweetest part of aging." As she said this, she was swimming laps in an effort to stay healthy and robust and ward off whatever it was she thought was *not* the sweetest part of aging.

GOLDEN RULES OF GRANDPARENTING

1. Trust your children who have just become parents.

They know more than you think they do, and they have the same powerful parental instincts you had.

2. Even if you have some doubts, don't display them. Act as if you trust them more than perhaps you do.

You may think that boy who continually kept you up while he missed curfew or that girl who cried her eyes out and didn't want to go to school because her hair didn't look right could never grow up to be a responsible parent, but don't let those old impressions blind you or affect the way you react to your son or daughter now.

When you disagree with a parenting decision, don't blurt out the first thing that comes to mind. Swallow. Count to ten. Excuse yourself and go for a little walk.

3. Follow the parents' lead.

No matter how much you think you know, and no matter how much you're willing to do, it is ultimately their way or the highway. And if you can't help having conflicting opinions, you'll do much better if you don't express them too quickly or too often. Today's parents will have some parenting theories that seem foreign to you, but you don't want to be the person who says, "When you were a baby, we did it the old-fashioned way."

4. Ask what you need to know, but exude confidence.

Parents want to feel that their baby is in good hands with you. Strollers and cribs and toys may have changed, but you are still an experienced caretaker. Don't be afraid to ask questions, but remember to be confident in your own abilities.

5. Respect your relationship with each new parent.

If you are the mother of the new mommy, your relationship might make her more disposed to follow advice based on your own experience, especially during pregnancy. If you are the mother-in-law, it is even more important that you respect the new mother. These infamous in-law relationships can be a great source of strain on both your child and his or her spouse—during what is already one of the most trying times of their lives. Remember to respond to the boundaries the new parents create. As all of you learn, understand, and accept your role in this new baby's life, you will become an effective team. And if you remain a consistent, open-minded, non-judgmental source of comfort and support, it will pay off in the long run.

6. Enjoy who you are at this very moment.

Having raised your own children, you know how quickly the time goes. One minute our children are teetering along taking their first steps, and the next minute they're asking to borrow the car or crossing a stage to receive a diploma. People often say the best thing about being a grandparent is that you have a really great visit *and then you hand them back*. But my hunch is you will want more of them. You will be sorry to see them go when the visit is over. This is not your "job" as it was with your own children, so instead of trying to take on more responsibility than necessary, revel in the experience of grandparenthood.

CHAPTER 2

Arrival (Newborn)

WHAT'S STILL TRUE

Life begins with an APGAR

If your children were born after 1952, they likely were given an APGAR test one minute after birth and then again five minutes later. That is still the trusted method of evaluating a newborn. Named after Virginia Apgar, an anesthesiologist who developed the scoring system to assess the effect of obstetric anesthesia on newborns, the test quickly evaluates a newborn's condition in five areas:

1. Appearance (skin coloration)
2. Pulse (heart rate)
3. Grimace response (or "reflex irritability")
4. Activity and muscle tone
5. Respiration (breathing rate and effort)

Each category is worth two points—so the maximum score is ten.

A score below seven signals to doctors that the baby may need immediate care, but the test does not predict long-term health. Cesarean birth, premature birth, or complicated delivery may lead to lower APGAR scores.

A few words about early babies

Not all babies are born at precisely nine months—or forty weeks, which is now the term commonly applied to full-term pregnancies. In fact, only about 4–5 percent of babies are born at that forty-week "due date." Approximately 60 percent are born within a week on either side of the due date. However, about 12 percent of babies are born prematurely—earlier than thirty-seven weeks—and only about 2 percent of babies are born before they reach thirty-two weeks. These babies typically have "low birth weight," considered to be less than five pounds, eight ounces.

> ## RELIABLE SOURCES OF INFORMATION
>
> If your grandchild is born pre-term or with low birth weight, you'll want to get much more information from sources such as http://www.stanfordchildrens.org/en/topic/default?id=prematurity-90-P02401 and http://www.marchofdimes.org/baby/premature-babies.aspx. Some good tips for grandparents of premature babies are available at http://www.marchofdimes.org/baby/grandparents-and-the-nicu.aspx.

There is very good news about the survival rate and the outlook for babies born prematurely, with outcomes that are dramatically different from what they were thirty years ago. Medical science has made major advances in caring for these babies. Over the past decades, some babies born weighing less than one pound have survived and done quite well. For many premature babies, it takes time to "catch up," but, happily, it happens.

Usually, care for pre-term babies is given in a NICU (neonatal intensive care unit) by specialists known as neonatologists until the baby is ready to go home, which can be a few days, a few weeks, or longer. Problems typically experienced by pre-term babies may include breathing, digestive system issues, vision, apnea (temporary pause in breathing), infections, anemia, and jaundice.

Extreme hygiene is very important in the NICU, so sometimes only parents are allowed to visit. Visiting hours are usually liberal, even around the clock. Some hospitals let parents designate a few other visitors, which can include grandparents. If so, you could sit in the NICU for the baby's parents while they get some rest. Whether or not you're able to visit, you can still play a crucial role by helping with the baby's siblings or the family's pets, home, or other daily life necessities. It is a difficult start for new parents, especially if the pre-term birth was unexpected, so the family needs to pull together.

My middle son—born not prematurely but with other issues—lived in a NICU and then a PICU (pediatric intensive care unit) for several months before coming home. The real heroes of that experience were the nurses. They were supportive, patient, kind, and very professional. It takes a special kind of person to work in a NICU.

The other advice I have is to encourage your son or daughter and their spouse to get their pre-term baby to the best, most qualified hospital possible, even if it requires a transfer by special ambulance.

The newborn adjusts to life outside the womb

At birth the baby starts to get oxygen from his or her own lungs instead of from the placenta and the mother's bloodstream. Most babies accomplish this in the first sixty seconds of life. The baby also must begin to regulate his or her own body temperature. This may take a little time, so babies are often placed in a warm incubator.

The American Academy of Pediatrics recommends that all newborns be examined for jaundice, which is caused by a buildup of bilirubin in the blood. Bilirubin comes from the breakdown of red blood cells, and the immature liver of an infant commonly can't process all the bilirubin. This condition often becomes apparent within the first few days of birth and can be resolved shortly after. If medical professionals at the hospital notice signs of jaundice, the newborn may be placed in a bed under a bilirubin light. If the baby is already home after the first few days of being born, parents and grandparents can look for signs of yellowish skin or eyes.

Newborns are "beautiful"—no matter how they look

You must have had a beautiful baby. I did, too. But we probably weren't objective with our own babies, and we won't be objective about this new little grandbaby either. Still, we may notice a few things—most of which are only temporary and perfectly normal.

The baby's head may be oddly shaped—long and narrow, short and wide, or not perfectly symmetrical. The sections of skull in a baby's head are flexible to pass through the birth canal. The skull becomes more rigid in the coming weeks.

Newborns often have puffy eyes—in some cases so puffy that the baby can't really open them until the puffiness recedes. And the color of their eyes may change. A baby's eyes can take six months or longer to show their true color.

The baby's skin may appear bruised, blotchy, or blemished. Bruises during birth come from forceps or bumping into the mother's pelvic bone. Skin conditions can range from red rashes to tiny white spots to yellowish, seedy-looking bumps. These go away in a matter of days or weeks. Birthmarks are different and may last longer. If you want to know more about identifying them, the Mayo Clinic offers an online slideshow with descriptions of birthmarks: http://www.mayoclinic.org/birthmarks/sls-20076683.

Did your grandbaby get your full, lush head of hair, or Granddad's receding hairline? Too soon to tell. Some babies are born with a lot of hair and some are born with none at all. Often, newborn hair falls out in the next weeks and months, and "real" hair grows in. It's almost certain that babies get less bald as time goes on, unlike Granddad. Hair color, like eye color, often changes in the weeks and months following birth.

Other bodily occurrences

WEIGHT: Babies usually lose weight right after birth and recover within the second week.

HERNIA: A hernia or protrusion in the groin area or near the belly button is not unusual. An umbilical cord hernia will typically close on its own. The other kind, called an inguinal hernia, is located in the lower abdomen or groin area and sometimes requires surgery. For more information on hernias: http://www.kidshealth.org/parent/system/surgical/hernia.html.

TONGUE-TIE: Another common condition is when a baby's tongue is a little too attached by a cord to the floor of his/her mouth. This can either have no effect, or it can affect breast-feeding, swallowing, and eventually talking. The connecting membrane is called a frenulum, so the relatively minor procedure to correct the condition is called a frenotomy. Your grandbaby's parents may decide to have it done right away in the hospital or wait to see if and how the baby is affected.

LANUGO: Some infants are born with a lot of hair (called lanugo) on their body. This falls off within a few days.

SECRETIONS: You may notice secretions from the newborn's breasts or from a baby girl's vagina. This results from the high level of the estrogen hormone during pregnancy. The secretions will stop within the first few weeks.

MECONIUM: Don't be alarmed if your grandbaby excretes stringy, greenish-black waste at first. This is called "meconium" and will soon pass out of your grandbaby's system.

WHAT'S NEW

You might be surprised by just how much has changed about how parents now nurture and protect newborns, from medical tests to driving laws to sleeping positions. Now, as a grandparent, you can take full advantage of the information that wasn't available when we were raising our children.

Doctors now test newborns for more than forty disorders before they leave the hospital. I want you to know this because I didn't. My son and I were communicating mostly through voice mail and at one point he left a message that said, "We might leave the hospital tomorrow or the next day because they need to do another round of tests." I had no immediate way of asking him or finding out, "Tests for what? Is there a problem?" I was worried until I found out these tests are now routine. All babies get tested—and not because the doctors suspect there is a problem. Screening requirements vary from state to state, but all are aimed at identifying rare illnesses for which early treatment is vital.

YOU MAY HEAR THESE TERMS AND NOT KNOW WHAT THEY MEAN

CORD BLOOD BANKING: Although still relatively uncommon, some parents choose to "bank" an infant's cord blood so it will available for future stem cell transplants. If the cord blood is stored in a public bank, it can be used to help anyone who needs it. In a private bank, the cord blood is saved in case a family member needs it. The American Academy of

Pediatrics encourages donations to public cord blood banks and suggests donations to private banks only when an older sibling already has a condition that may need a stem cell transplant.

DOULAS: You're probably familiar with midwives and labor coaches, but doulas are another kind of professional that may play an important role in the birth of your grandchild. The word *doula* comes from an ancient Greek word that means "woman who serves." Doulas assist the mother and father pre-birth, during birth, and post-partum. I've heard them described as a mother's "comrade" or a "birth guide." In some cases, they work to support the pregnant woman's desire to have a natural birth. Through breathing exercises, relaxation techniques, suggestions for labor positions, massage, and hypnosis, a doula seeks to maximize the mother's birth experience. Proponents of doulas point to studies showing that women supported with doulas are less likely to require Cesarean sections, induced labor, or pain medication.

LACTATION COOKIES: Many recipes have been developed for cookies containing ingredients intended to increase milk supply in a nursing mother. These key ingredients are oats, brewer's yeast, wheat germ, and flaxseed. I could not find medical information to support this claim, other than these cookies tend to be high in iron, protein, B vitamins, zinc, and complex carbohydrates—all of which boost health in general. They also contain galactagogues (now there's a new word, sounding like "stalagmites" or something else found in a cave . . .) purported to promote lactation in humans and animals.

More is known about the benefits of breastfeeding

As better infant formulas were developed in the 1970s and 1980s, bottle feeding became more convenient and, consequently, more popular. But many experts now agree that breast milk transfers important antibodies to an infant. Plus, breastfeeding is linked to many benefits for mothers and may help women lose the "baby weight" and reduce the chance of post-partum depression and certain cancers. The American Academy of Pediatrics recommends breastfeeding exclusively for the first six months. That being said, if a mother chooses not to breastfeed, the formulas available today closely replicate mother's milk. While breastfeeding provides a wonderful way to bond, so does snuggling an infant with a bottle. Your daughter or daughter-in-law will choose what is best for her and her baby.

It's illegal to ride in a car holding a baby on your lap

Every state has child restraint laws, and many hospitals won't discharge a baby without a properly installed car seat in the car. Some states require that a certified Child Passenger Safety Technician (CPST) check the installation at a permanent inspection station, but parents may choose to do this anyway (visit http://www.safekids.org for locations). Thirty years ago, infant seats were usually strapped into the passenger seat where we could entertain our babies as we drove. That was probably never advisable—and it's now illegal. Today's baby seat is rear-facing and placed in the backseat. How do you know what your grandbaby is doing back there? Install one of the many popular mirrors now on the market for that exact purpose.

Babies are no longer put on their tummies to sleep

In the mid-1980s, research linked tummy sleeping to higher incidences of SIDS (Sudden Infant Death Syndrome). By 1992, the American Academy of Pediatrics advised against tummy sleeping. Some experts and parents agree that babies often don't sleep as well on their backs because their startle reflex seems to wake them more often, but back sleeping is proven to be much safer.

To reduce the risk of SIDS, it's also important to avoid:

- Keeping the room too stuffy and too warm. A temperature of around 68 degrees is recommended.
- Soft bedding. Blankets, pillows, quilts, etc., should stay out of the baby's bed for the first year of life.
- Smoking. Exposure to secondhand smoke raises the risk of SIDS because chemicals in secondhand smoke may interfere with the way the infant's brain regulates breathing.

However, there are a few risk factors that can't be controlled, such as ethnicity (Native American and African

American babies have a higher incidence of SIDS), family history, and serotonin deficiency (there's currently no way to test for this deficiency).

Babies are often wrapped like burritos

One of the remedies developed to calm a newborn's startle reflex during back sleeping is the swaddling technique, in which a baby's arms are tucked snugly at his or her sides. Most hospitals teach new parents this technique, and the parents can teach you if they want you to use it. Swaddling can be done with a blanket or one of the special Velcro suits available at baby stores. You will know you have done the job well if the baby looks like a burrito.

A swaddled baby must *never* sleep on his tummy. A baby who is able to turn from his back to his tummy should never be swaddled. The American Academy of Pediatrics recommends that you stop swaddling when the baby is two months old. The baby's legs should not be tightly swaddled because they need to move their hips for normal development.

MORE ABOUT HEALTHY SWADDLING

For more facts and a video on swaddling that doesn't harm hips: http://www.hipdysplasia.org/developmental-dysplasia-of-the-hip/hip-healthy-swaddling/.

WHAT YOU CAN DO

If you are invited to share the first moments, hours, or days of your new grandchild's life, you are very lucky indeed. If you live near enough, your first role might be taking care of things at the house—feeding pets, running errands, building the crib—while the new parents are at the hospital. When you do get your hands on that baby (you've taken care of your immunizations, right?), remember to support the baby's head and neck. It takes about four weeks for a newborn to build enough muscle to hold up that big, beautiful head!

You're joining a new web of relationships

Unless you are the only grandparent—and there are no aunts, uncles, or cousins—you will be part of a web of relationships with your grandchild at the center. In spite of their best intentions, some grandparents feel a little jealous if other relatives are closer, more available, or more financially advantaged. Of course, the baby is oblivious to all this. And hopefully, family members will share time and attention without resentment. Here is some advice from experts on how to integrate successfully into the family network:

- Honesty is good—but some things are better left unsaid.
- Don't criticize the baby's parents in front of other relatives—only compliment them.
- Don't criticize the other grandparents.
- Don't criticize your son- or daughter-in-law in conversations with your child.
- Respect the rules and routines the parents set. Don't be the one who does exactly what the parents asked you not to—even if you think you know better.

- Be true to yourself. Develop a special bond with your grandchild based on who you really are. Don't think you have to "compete" with other relatives.
- If you have a concern you think needs addressing, request a time to talk with the parents. Speak in a non-threatening manner and avoid sounding critical. Ask questions and listen before you give your own opinion. Tread gently.
- Let your genuine love shine through—for all of the members of your grandbaby's family.

One young mother told me how happy she was that her parents and her husband's parents had begun to see each other socially occasionally—outside of their times with the younger generation. They were able to form a friendship and move toward seeing themselves as part of the same family. Sometimes the grandmothers get together for lunch or some combination of grandparents join in a round of golf. If you can make that effort, it might be worth it.

Your relationships with those of your friends who are also grandparents may take on a new dimension. After I became a grandmother, I adopted this rule: Never, ever ignore or underplay a friend's grandchild. You miss the potential for strengthening your friendship. Once you are a grandparent, you understand how good another person's interest in your family feels—and how bad indifference feels. Parents and grandparents love to talk about new additions to the family, show their pride, and share exciting news, milestones, and photos.

What new babies like

New babies like cuddles and physical contact. Soft and rhythmic sounds, including quiet talking and singing, comfort newborns who are more accustomed to the sounds inside their mothers' wombs. And studies show that they like the higher pitch and slower pace many adults instinctively use when talking to babies. Within a few days, newborns' eyes will begin to focus on objects about eight to fifteen inches away. One of their favorite sights will be human faces—including grandparent faces, of course! And if you're ever at a loss for how to pacify a newborn, gentle rocking and swaying is an excellent starting point. I got so used to swaying with my children that now when I hold my grandchild—or a dog or a cat—I automatically sway.

Infants remind us that life begins in innocence and simplicity. They have no agenda beyond surviving and thriving. Those of us who run around madly with to-do lists and commitments need only to rock with a sleeping infant to realize the meaning of time well spent.

I Am So New

As you fold your arms around me,
feel the beating of my heart,
the patience of my breath
as I settle into being held.
Watch my soft skin
mold around every expression
as I dream, startle, stretch, awaken—
unaware you are there.
See my eyes open and blink,
studying lights and shadows
and patterns that mean nothing yet.
I will learn in time
about sunshine and storms,
smiles and fears,
heaven and earth
But for now—
Spend time with me.
Hold me close.
Wonder at my new beginning.
Allow me to be who I am
in this very moment.

CHAPTER 3
Adjustments (0–3 Months)

POSSIBLE MILESTONES

- Lifting head briefly when on tummy
- Holding head steady when upright
- Focusing on a face
- Cooing, squealing, laughing
- Reacting to or turning toward sounds
- Beginning to reach for an object and trying to grasp it
- Bringing hands together
- Smiling, often randomly

WHAT'S STILL TRUE

It's a full-time job being a newborn

You might remember that new babies generally just eat and sleep during the first weeks of life. But there's more going on than you might imagine. A newborn has six states of consciousness: quiet awake, active alert, crying, drowsiness, active sleep, and quiet sleep.

In the **quiet awake** state, babies tend to watch and listen. The amount of time infants spend in this state increases as time goes on. By one month, it's typical to be in this state for about two and a half hours a day.

In the **active alert** state, arms wave and legs kick. This state is often a precursor to fussiness, and close on the heels of fussiness can come crying.

Babies are famous for the **crying** state. And although it's usually a result of hunger, discomfort, exhaustion, or unhappiness, it is often difficult for parents—and grandparents—to figure out which one is the problem at any particular moment!

Drowsiness in an infant looks much like it looks in anyone else: drooping eyelids, unfocused stare, yawns, stretches. Drowsiness usually shows up, of course, right before or right after sleep.

During **active sleep**, also known as REM sleep for "rapid eye movement," babies often move restlessly and make small noises. Babies spend about half of their sleep time in active sleep, and observers report that babies typically alternate between active and quiet sleep about every thirty minutes.

Quiet sleep . . . ahhhh. Babies in this state of sleep move less and breathe more regularly. The baby seems to have "zonked out." It is usually the most relaxed state for parents, too.

When you add up the time a newborn spends sleeping each day, in whatever state, the total is typically around sixteen or seventeen hours. But that time is broken up into many segments, usually no longer than two to four hours, sometimes much shorter.

And as you remember from raising your own children, responding to the needs of a newborn involves nonstop activity and plenty of confusion: "Why is she crying?" and "What should we do for him?" The unpredictability keeps parents hopping. That reality you cannot change. But being an extra pair of hands and a source of moral support can be a major help.

Babies seem fragile at first

Handling an infant again if you haven't had the chance in recent years might make you a little nervous at first, but you'll feel comfortable again in no time. In some cultures, a baby is tied to the mother's body almost constantly for the first few months or weeks. In our culture, babies are picked up and put down a lot. Some experts suggest avoiding sudden movement, such as swooping the baby up and handing the baby around to different people. They suggest gently touching the baby first, then carefully supporting the baby by slipping your hands under him or her and keeping your hands there for several seconds before you start lifting.

Putting the baby down without waking him or her up is another skill that might need refreshing. Check out the height of the crib mattress and the crib railing. Bending over a high railing to place the baby on a low mattress may require strength or flexibility you don't have. Make sure you can easily get out of the chair you use for rocking or feeding the baby. As you put your grandchild down, try to make the release gradual. Keep your hands on the baby, and keep singing if you've been singing until the baby has a chance to quiet.

Babies are noisy little beings

Since newborns spend so much time sleeping, you might spend your time together watching your grandchild sleep. You may notice a lot of stirring and startling, some grunting and twitching. In REM sleep, they are the most active. They also may experience what is called "periodic breathing," which means they might breathe rapidly, then pause, then resume breathing. This is common. During non-REM sleep, they are usually more peaceful. As the weeks go on, babies usually spend more time in non-REM sleep than REM sleep. In addition, many babies have some nasal congestion for four to six weeks after birth—not from a cold but from living in a liquid environment for all those months.

Just like your own children, your grandchild may get the hiccups. Watching a baby hiccup is probably a lot more uncomfortable than actually being that baby. If the baby has swallowed air while feeding, some additional sucking may help. If the baby is overstimulated, soothing might help.

Babies still need to be burped after feeding, and the positions recommended for burping haven't changed:

- Baby is against your chest with his/her head near your shoulder, rub upward or pat gently.
- Baby is sitting on your lap with your hands supporting him/her in front, rub upward or pat gently.
- Baby is lying facedown on your lap, rub upward or pat gently.

No matter how well they are burped, most babies spit up—either a little or a lot, occasionally or frequently. Typically, spitting up diminishes after the first six to nine months. As long as the baby doesn't have significant coughing or gagging and as long as the baby is still gaining weight, don't worry. Just keep a little cloth handy.

Colic still affects some infants

If you had a baby with colic, you probably haven't forgotten the symptoms. Babies with colic tend to cry or get extremely fussy for an extended period of time, often in the late afternoon or evening, although they seem perfectly comfortable at other times. Colic is as hard on parents these days as it was a generation ago. Typically the colicky kind of crying starts to occur around two to three weeks, peaks at around six weeks, and begins to diminish around twelve weeks. Some medical experts believe colic can be brought on by overstimulation and recommend taking the baby into a quiet room with low light and soothing him/her. Other possible causes of colic include feeding problems or an immature digestive system or exposure to secondhand smoke.

These days, you also may hear about "reflux"—a normal phenomenon that happens because the baby's esophageal sphincter doesn't tighten until around six months. It's estimated that half of all babies experience some reflux during the first few months of life, beginning around two weeks of age, and it may continue until around eighteen months. The official name is gastroesophageal reflux (GER). Typically, GER makes babies fussy intermittently through the day or all the time. What's happening is that reflux can feel like heartburn, so babies with that symptom may cry during and shortly after feeding and may arch their backs and look in other ways as if they are in pain. Often sleep problems accompany GER. Your son or daughter and their partner probably will know there are some suggested ways to alleviate reflux, such as keeping baby upright more of the time and having him/her sleep in a slightly inclined position. Smaller, more frequent meals may also help.

> ## IS IT GER OR GERD?
>
> There's a difference between GER and GERD (gastroesophageal reflux disease). GERD is a more serious type of reflux condition that causes more pervasive feeding problems and other symptoms that may include excessive gagging, choking, respiratory problems, failure to gain weight, and others. GERD warrants medical attention.

Basic care for newborns

THE UMBILICAL CORD STUMP: The advice used to be to dab on rubbing alcohol with a cotton swab during each diaper change. Now many doctors say to leave it alone. Do turn down the top of the diaper so it doesn't rub against the stump. Typically, it will heal and fall off within one to four weeks.

DIAPER CHANGES: Normal solid waste for boys or girls comes in various shades of yellow, green, or brown. If it's red or mucousy, point it out to the parents, a caregiver, or a doctor.

DIAPER CHANGES FOR BOYS: For a circumcised baby boy, it's generally advised to apply a small amount of petroleum jelly to the circumcision while it's healing (usually about three to four days). For an uncircumcised baby boy, just clean with a wipe as usual. Don't try to pull the foreskin back. The foreskin typically pulls pack on its own by the time a little boy is five years old.

DIAPER CHANGES FOR GIRLS: Wipe front to back and clean every crease. Wiping back to front can cause a bladder infection because solid waste has bacteria that urine doesn't.

TAKING A TEMPERATURE: The parents will probably be the ones taking the baby's temperature, but it's a good thing to know about, just in case. You were probably hoping that, over the past decades, someone invented something better than a rectal thermometer. Sorry, it didn't happen. But they now come in a digital variety and register a temperature in about a minute. The general advice is to insert the thermometer about one inch into the anus and wait one minute. You can remember it as the "one-for-one rule." Other methods aren't as accurate. For example, ear thermometers yield different results depending on the angle of the thermometer. After the baby is a year old, it won't matter that the reading be accurate to a tenth of a degree, so you will have other choices.

When you were a parent, you may have worried about high fevers causing brain damage. Your son or daughter will probably still worry, but here's some reassurance: While fevers of 108 degrees or more can cause brain damage, infections don't cause fevers that high. That kind of temperature results from hyperthermia (for example, if a baby is left in a hot car) but not infections.

WHAT'S NEW

Baby "essentials" aren't what they used to be

My favorite modern baby item: warm wipes. A little device sits near the changing table to supply perfectly warmed wipes. It feels so much kinder to change a diaper with a nice, soft, warm wipe instead of the chilly ones we used to use. And baby powder is definitely out, because some babies inhale it. Gone is that clean baby smell we all associated with baby powder.

White noise is popular these days. It's a gentle, consistent sound that muffles sharper, unexpected noises. White noise machines are now built into plush toys, such as lambs. They are designed to mimic the comforting sounds of mommy's womb. Even the hum of a fan or a washing machine or a hair dryer can provide the right kind of background noise to help a baby sleep.

TODAY'S SUPER SWINGS

Remember the wind-up or battery-operated swings that occupied our babies on occasion? Today's swings are new and improved. Now they swing side-to-side and front-to back. And some of them also vibrate.

Cribs have become much safer over the past twenty years. No more drop-down sides. The slats are closer together. With all these changes, many regulated by law to prevent suffocation and choking hazards, the crib you've been saving in the attic may not be a very good idea. Crib bumpers are now considered hazardous. If a baby is able to rise on all fours in the crib or come close to reaching a mobile, the mobile should be removed.

There's good news about childhood diseases

In the past twenty-five years, some serious diseases have become much rarer among American children. Hopefully, your grandchild's parents have done their research and are making informed decisions. The Centers for Disease Control, American Academy of Pediatrics, the National Academy of Medicine (formerly the Institute of Medicine), and the American Academy of Family Physicians have approved the current immunization schedule of twenty-five shots in the first fifteen months of life. These shots immunize against whooping cough (pertussis), diphtheria, tetanus, mumps, measles, rubella, rotavirus (given orally), polio, hepatitis B, and other diseases. If your grandbaby's parents are concerned about immunizations, they should talk about their concerns with their pediatrician. Some questions about immunizations are advancing from the medical field to the legal arena as some states take steps to make immunizations mandatory for school children.

The chickenpox vaccine is a particularly significant advance. You probably remember as I do the way chickenpox would run through schools and families. With an incubation period stretching from fourteen to twenty-one days and a contagious period that could run from two days before the rash appeared all the way until the blisters had scabs, some mothers even made an effort to expose all the children in the family at once. The new chickenpox vaccine debuted in 1995. Until then, approximately 11,000 people were hospitalized with chickenpox every year and as many as one hundred died. The first shot is now recommended at twelve to fifteen months with a booster between ages four and six.

Sterilizing items is less mandatory now

Common wisdom now suggests that new items like bottle nipples be sterilized before the first use for five minutes in boiling water. But after that, those items can simply be washed with hot, soapy water and rinsed well. This will be a relief to those of us who would start the items boiling, get distracted, and end up with nipples and pacifier rings welded to the bottom of an empty pan because all the water had boiled away.

One of my friends told me his wife, the mother of three boys, progressed down the sterilizing spectrum with their children and their pacifiers. According to him, with the first son, she'd sterilize the pacifier each time it fell on the ground. With the second, she'd run it under hot water. With the third, she'd wipe it off on her jeans and give it back to him. (But I think he was kidding.)

Solid food is being started later

Our mothers told us (and we probably believed it) that a baby with a full stomach would sleep better and that solids (usually rice cereal) would help satisfy a baby's hunger beginning at about six weeks. The American Academy of Pediatrics now recommends that breastfed babies have exclusively breast milk for the first six months. Babies fed with formula should wait until at least four months before starting any solids. Studies have shown that breast milk and formula actually provide more calories than solid food—and babies cannot digest or properly swallow solids before then.

Parenting philosophies have changed

Do you remember researching and following a specific theory of parenting when you were raising young children? I don't. For me, it was more following the model of my mother and my older sister and listening to my maternal instincts—and maybe turning now and then to the Dr. Benjamin Spock book or the Dr. T. Berry Brazelton book. Today, with so much information available to parents and with a body of work on child development that is so much more extensive, parenting philosophies have proliferated. Each has its proponents and detractors. Your son or daughter and their partner may choose to follow one approach or another, combine certain elements, or make up their own. It affects you as a grandparent because if your desire is to align your own actions to the wishes and expectations of your grandchild's parents, their philosophies will influence what you do. The chart on page 50 gives a brief overview of some current philosophies, but I'd like to say more about the two that I think are especially interesting.

Attachment parenting is an approach your daughter or son and their partner might choose as their parenting guide. Some of its practices may seem new or different to you, but if you learn about them and understand them, you can think through the ways and to what degree you are able to follow them.

In attachment parenting, parents base their actions on the idea that babies learn to trust and thrive when their needs early in life are consistently met by a caregiver. Few people who love a baby would disagree with that idea. While advocates don't always completely agree on precisely what constitutes attachment parenting, they tend to agree that the parenting style is "child-centered" and not structured for the convenience of the parents. The following practices are usually part of attachment parenting:

- Breastfeeding—and letting the baby set the feeding schedule (whether breastfed or bottle fed).

- Baby-wearing, which means holding or carrying a baby much of the time to create closeness.
- Sleeping close to the baby at night, either in the same room or even in the same bed—sometimes called "co-sleeping." (Some experts caution against sleeping in the same bed because of possible risks associated with a small baby sleeping with large parents.)
- Providing constant loving care (from a limited number of caregivers) and responding quickly and consistently to cues from the infant.

Mothers are generally at the center of attachment parenting, primarily because of breastfeeding, which happens day and night. The baby's dad can participate in all the other aspects, and you can, too. Experts agree that a close relationship with a grandparent can add to a child's feeling of security.

Your daughter or son and their partner hold the key to these decisions. If they invite you into that small circle of caregivers, you will need to agree to the practices. For example, when you care for the baby at naptime or bedtime, you most likely will hold the baby or lie down with him/her instead of using a bassinet or crib. You can see that this requires a great deal of time and commitment from the parents or caregiver.

Mindful parenting is a choice you can make about the way you, personally, view and respond to your grandchild. Mindfulness as a philosophy extends way beyond interacting with an infant and can be applied to relating to the world in general and to all the people you encounter in it.

Mindfulness has very old roots—yes, *even* older than any grandparent alive today. It is a mind-body practice, based on ancient Zen Buddhist meditation techniques. It has a spiritual foundation but does not conflict with other religions. Simply put, mindfulness involves paying attention to the experience of the present moment, deliberately and non-judgmentally.

In the 1960s, the concepts of mindfulness began to creep into American consciousness, and the Beatles' interest in transcendental meditation was one of the reasons. In the 1970s, a number of forward-thinking scientists began using mindfulness and meditation in various healing therapies, and Jon Kabat-Zinn, now an author and professor of medicine emeritus at the University of Massachusetts, developed a program called Mindfulness-Based Stress Reduction (or MBSR).

The mindfulness concepts, phrased in different ways by different scholars, include non-judging, patience, beginner's mind (not letting what we "know" prevent us from seeing things as they really are), trust, non-striving, acceptance, and letting go.

In 1997, Kabat-Zinn and his wife, Myla, an experienced childbirth educator and birthing assistant, applied the concepts to parenting in a book entitled *Everyday Blessings*. In this book, they stress sovereignty (each human being respected for his or her true nature), empathy, and acceptance.

The Kabat-Zinns's book is subtitled "The Inner Work of Mindful Parenting," and it *is* work, particularly for busy, stressed-out, and multitasking parents who spend countless hours with their child and juggle many other demands. For grandparents, because we want so much for our relationship with our grandchild to be positive and meaningful, and perhaps because the time we spend is limited and precious, mindful *grandparenting* seems to suit our best instincts.

Mindfulness has many dimensions, and to really practice it you will want to do more research—but to give you just a taste, it involves pausing before you act or react and being aware in a non-judgmental way of how things really are. In their book, the Kabat-Zinns compare a mindful parent (or, in our case, grandparent) to a towering oak tree in a storm—a calm, supportive presence for a child. Even in the most challenging times, mindfulness helps us to take a step back and ask, "What is truly important here?"

As we look back on our parenting years, we might see that some of our parental instincts led us down those paths, but perhaps not perfectly. There were other forces at work, too: wanting to have a "good," well-behaved child, a socially gregarious child, an athlete, a high achiever—and now and then we wanted many things in the same child, all at once. Did we know how to take time to pause, see things as they really were, and choose the most appropriate and nurturing response?

When I now read about mindfulness and apply it to grandparenting, I think, "Fantastic. Second chance!" This time, I won't be in such a hurry to get someplace with my grandchild—either literally or metaphorically.

Many parents combine elements of different techniques. Some now collaborate with parenting coaches in order to implement different strategies. Your best approach to this issue is open-minded support and confidence. Discuss the different methods with your grandbaby's parents so that you can avoid behavior that conflicts with their principles.

A parent's approach to his or her role in this new baby's life is made up of hundreds of decisions. Here are some of the new philosophies you may hear about and resources for learning more:

Parenting philosophies	Characteristics
Unconditional Parenting	Traditional methods of rewards and punishments teach a child that he or she is loved only when they impress us. Offers alternatives. (Alfie Kohn, http://www.alfiekohn.org/UP)
Conscious Parenting	A set of beliefs about how children thrive. Involves making deliberate choices about raising children and gaining a better understanding of the knowledge and memories from your own parents and childhood. (Lee Lozowick's book *Conscious Parenting*)
Intentional Parenting	Emphasizes being purposeful about what you do with a child, setting aside time, inviting connection. Sometimes includes Christian perspective. (http://www.theintentionallife.com/nine-habits-of-an-intentional-parent)
Positive Parenting	Favors positive guidance over forms of discipline. (http://www.ahaparenting.com/parenting-tools/positive-discipline/positive-discipline)

RIE – Resources for Infant Educarers	Demonstrating respect for babies every time we interact with them. Some similarities to mindful parenting. (https://www.rie.org/educaring /ries-basic-principles)
Authoritarian, Authoritative, Permissive, and Uninvolved Parenting	Observations by psychologist Diana Baumrind on styles that vary in levels of control/demandness and support/responsiveness. (http://www.psychology.about.com /od/developmentalpsychology/a /parenting-style.htm)
Free-Range Parenting	Doesn't apply to babies, but free-range parents believe in giving their children the same kind of freedom that used to be more common—letting young children walk alone, ride public transportation, or play in parks without a parent or caregiver nearby, etc. (Lenore Skenazy's book *Free-Range Kids: Giving Our Kids the Freedom We Had Without Going Nuts with Worry*)

WHAT YOU CAN DO

Start talking!

During the first three months of life, your grandbaby's brain is developing at a rapid rate. From birth through the third year of life, a human brain grows to about 90 percent of its adult capacity. What's happening is sometimes called "brain wiring." Connections between brain cells are being made constantly. These connections are forged until around age ten or eleven, when the brain becomes more selective and discards any connections that are rarely used.

Experts now urge adults to communicate with their babies from the very beginning. Make it a habit to talk often—about anything. It doesn't matter what you say; it just matters that the baby is hearing human voices. Talk about what you're doing and what's in front of you, and give names to objects and body parts. Change your pitch and tone of voice periodically. Remember that reading and singing are just as helpful as talking. But know when to take a break. A baby who has had enough will look away, turn away, or get fussy.

"Talk, read, and sing" and "Too Small to Fail"

Based on what is now known about child development, encouraging parents to talk, read, and sing to their children has become the focus for several well-respected, high-powered organizations. For example, Hillary Clinton and the Clinton Foundation are partnering with Next Generation, an innovative nonprofit organization, on an initiative called "Too Small to Fail." Its main priority is closing the "word gap," the striking disparity in the vocabularies of young children from higher-income families versus those from lower-income families. Research shows that by age four, children from lower-income families have heard up to 30,000,000 fewer words than their higher-income peers. This gap in hearing words translates directly into a gap in learning words. Children whose parents (and grandparents!) talk, read, and sing to them from an early age arrive at school with significantly larger vocabularies than children who don't have that kind of early interaction.

But don't forget to listen! Encourage your grandchild to talk back to you. When he or she begins to burble, respond as if it is the most fascinating thing you have ever heard. Because, really, it is. Ask questions, pause, and then answer. Imitate the sounds your grandbaby makes and then expand the conversation.

With my first son, now the parent of my first grandchild, I remember propping him up on a pillow when he was two months old and leaning toward him, eye to eye. He stared up at me with an intent expression and tried to make unintelligible sounds as if his life depended on it. My comments back to him were simple.

"Really?"

"What else?"

"Do you have more to say?"

Imagine how great it will be if your grandchild gets into the lifelong habit of *really* pouring his or her heart out to you—because you always listen!

Relationships in your family may change

With the arrival of this new grandchild, existing relationships may shift and new bonds may be formed, either intentionally or unintentionally. One of the more common topics of conversation among grandparents is the tricky "in-law" relationship. This includes the relationship with the parent who is not your son or daughter, as well as the relationship with his or her parents who share your grandparenting role. With the birth of a grandbaby, these relationships become more complex, and edges may appear that weren't obvious before.

I had heard friends of mine talk about "walking on eggshells," "not rocking the boat," "biting their tongues," and "knowing their place." It all seemed so negative, a roiling storm cloud in an otherwise sunny situation. It *can't* be that much of a problem, I thought. There must be some way to avoid those kinds of frustrations and disappointments. We are all adults, right? Do we have to become paranoid, conniving, and manipulative?

As simple and pure as your feelings for your grandbaby may be, that is not always true of the relationships among adults. Even if you had a close relationship before, the baby's arrival might make it more complicated.

Let's start with the most basic connection—and that is between you and your son or daughter's partner. Your daughter or son and their partner may or may not have included you in their lives and all of their decisions. You could probably achieve some distance and objectivity. You weren't, after all, eager to develop a relationship with that totally impractical, oversized, and overpriced white sectional they bought a while ago. But now there's a *baby* involved! There's much more at stake. Everyone around the baby wants to step into roles that will be special and meaningful for the baby and the parents. History, geography, and attitude all play a role—but the primary issue seems to be who gave birth to whom.

In-laws and out-laws

When there are two sets of grandparents (or more, if any of the grandparents have divorced and remarried), one tends to be the parents of the mother; the other, of the father. (Issues among the parents of same-sex partners may be similar, but for the sake of simplicity, we will use "mother" and "father.") Many people believe that the parents of the baby's mother are part of an inner circle, while the parents of the baby's father are part of an outer circle—or completely left out.

The logic behind this viewpoint is that the mother of the baby (especially if she's breastfeeding) is most often the primary caregiver. The bond between mothers and maternal grandmothers frequently grows closer than ever when the baby is born. Maybe the new mother feels safe asking her mother questions. Maybe she now realizes and appreciates more than ever what her mother did to raise her.

If the relationship between the mother of the baby and her mother is very close, and you are not that grandmother, you should come to terms with that fact. Set out to build your own unique relationship.

I've collected some advice from experienced paternal grandmothers to help keep things flowing smoothly with their daughters-in-law:

Be inclusive in your comments. Don't say things to your son that you wouldn't say to your daughter-in-law. Bite the bullet and say it to both, or don't say anything at all.

Try to remain neutral when disagreements occur instead of taking sides. Be the person who adds positive energy, not the person who stirs up arguments or feeds animosity. Think before you speak. No one likes to be criticized, judged, second-guessed, pre-empted, or underestimated.

Let things roll off your back. This first year of raising a child is, as you surely recall, one of the most stressful for parents. As the grandparent, you get to wave good-bye to your grandchild and go home—to a full night's sleep! But your grandchild's parents won't have that luxury. And new mothers are experiencing radical physical and hormonal changes at this time. An oversensitive grandparent is the last thing those new parents need. Remember that stress, confusion, and exhaustion will strain relationships. Don't add to that strain or create cracks that will be difficult to patch later.

Ask, don't assume. Whether it's dropping by for a visit or planning a holiday, respect the rights of this new family to have a life of their own and to make independent decisions.

Don't telegraph the wrong message. Don't let your desire to be helpful give the unintended impression that you think your grandchild's parents aren't doing a good job. When the baby first comes home from the hospital and you pitch in to unload the dishwasher, do a load of laundry, or take out the garbage, it is a big help. But if you continue to take on chores without their request, the new parents might feel that you find them disorganized, incapable, or incompetent.

Consideration gets better results than competition

Most successful grandparents agree that one of the worst things you can do is to get into some kind of competition with the other grandparents. Who can give the best gift? Get the baby's biggest smiles? Have the most overnight visits? It's treacherous territory. Respecting the other set of grandparents is by far the wiser course of action. If you have to, choose your battles. Better yet, have no battles.

What are some ways to show consideration?

Be alert to cues. When is it time to change the subject or bring the visit to a happy conclusion? A friend of mine explained that her grandchild's other grandmother was less physically active and "not interested in crawling around on the floor to play." She noted, "So when we're all there together, I tend not to do that either. I don't want to make her self-conscious." Finding ways to be kind and generous can prevent animosity from forming, especially when all of the relatives are assembled.

Remember to listen and empathize.

Resist the urge to be the one who always has the answers.

WHEN TO SPEAK UP

As much as you will try to "keep the peace," there are exceptions. If you know something or witness something that endangers the baby, you'll need to talk about it. For example, if the other grandparents have a dog that growls at the baby, a swimming pool gate they don't keep closed, or the habit of texting while they drive with the baby in the backseat—be brave, be as tactful as you can be, and speak up.

Most of these disagreements and jealousies stem from a lack of communication. Another friend of mine defused the problem proactively with what she called a friendly in-law summit, in which both sets of grandparents sat down together.

She said, "We explained what we hoped to have our role be, what holiday traditions were important to us, etc.—and the other grandparents did the same. We actually got to laughing about it. No one wanted Halloween."

Experts recommend clarity and honesty when it comes to creating your grandparenting role. How much time will you be available? What kinds of activities are best for you? Bedtime? Playtime? Visits for several hours or an entire weekend with your grandchild? How much financial help are you willing and able to provide? As soon as you answer these basic questions, you will have a better picture of the type of grandparent you want to become. It's important—for you and your grandchild—that you stay true to that role. Be yourself.

As you come to understand your own interests and desires, focus on the new parents' needs, too. What do they really need from their child's grandparents? Dependability and reassurance. They want to know they can count on you to do what you say you'll do, whether it's an occasional night of babysitting or more continuous support. They'll have doubts from time to time about their decisions and their own parenting skills and will look to you for reassurance. When you follow their lead, you're confirming that you have confidence in their abilities.

Family pets will need to adjust, too

The human members of your family aren't the only ones who will need to adjust to life with a baby—your pets will, too. A dog or cat living in the baby's home will have the biggest adjustment, but if your grandchild is going to visit your home, you'll want to reach some level of comfort when the baby and your pet are in the same house.

For dogs, experts suggest a visit to the groomer—including a bath and nail trim—as well as a check-up with the vet to make sure your dog is healthy and up-to-date with immunizations. If your dog needs a refresher on basic obedience, such as sit, stay, down, leave it, and drop it, you might want to put some effort toward that as you anticipate the birth day. After the baby is born, you might want to bring home some items that have the baby's smell on them and let your dog get used to that new smell.

When your grandchild comes into your house for the first time, it's wise to have a helper to attend to the dog if you'll be holding the baby. The helper will have your dog on a leash—but in a relaxed manner—and have treats on hand to reward good behavior. Try to keep the first interactions calm and positive and take little steps, such as having the dog sniff the baby's feet while you talk to the dog affectionately.

If you have a cat, you know cats can be contrary. However, there are some cat-related worries that you can put aside. First, pregnant women have long been advised to stay away from cat litter boxes because of a disease called toxoplasmosis. The extra caution may be a good idea, but the truth is that toxoplasmosis is much more often a result of eating undercooked meat. Second, there is a myth that cats try to smother babies. That's not true. But cats are usually more able than dogs to do things like jump into cribs, so you may want to make the room in your house where the baby sleeps when visiting off-limits to your cat. As with the dog, use treats and praise to keep the cat from feeling it's being punished because the new baby has arrived.

Some people want to go even further with preparing their pets, such as playing a recording of baby sounds so the dog or cat will get used to those sounds. If you don't want to go that far, you could have granddad go into the next room and pretend to be a baby. Just kidding. You'll find more good advice and information on the ASPCA web site (https://www.aspca.org/pet-care/virtual-pet-behaviorist/dog-behavior/introducing-your-dog-your-new-baby) and the Humane Society web site (http://www.humanesociety.org/animals/resources/tips/pets_babies.html).

What to have at your home

If you're open to the idea of having overnights at grandma's house, here's a list of basic equipment it's good to have on hand:

- Somewhere for the baby to sleep—a bassinet or crib, unless the parents bring their own portable
- Somewhere to change the baby—and all the supplies (diapers, wipes, petroleum jelly)
- A few sets of clothing
- A duplicate of the baby's favorite blanket or stuffed animal
- Pacifiers, if the baby uses them
- A baby first-aid book and the supplies recommended there, including a rectal thermometer and a medicinal syringe (to give medicine if necessary)

Your Smile

In its so new state,
your smile
opens the world
like an alternate route
in a traffic jam.
Your smile
clears the skies,
parts the waters,
lifts the shades,
changes my outlook.
Where does it come from—
that smile?
From purity and innocence,
harmony and joy.
Your smile is the cure
for too many emails
and too little sleep,
the morning rush,
the evening news.
Wars wouldn't start,
arguments would end,
mistakes would be forgotten
enemies, forgiven—
if they could just see
YOUR SMILE.

CHAPTER 4

Advances (3–6 Months)

POSSIBLE MILESTONES

- Sitting with steady head with support, later with less support
- Keeping head aligned with back when pulled to sitting
- Bearing some weight on legs and beginning to try to pull up
- Rolling over
- Grasping items and passing them from one hand to the other
- Attempting to hold a toy or object when you try to take it away
- Babbling, expanding range of sounds
- Smiling back when you smile
- Beginning to eat solid food
- Extending periods of continuous sleep at night

WHAT'S STILL TRUE

Children develop at different rates but in the same basic patterns.

Motor development in an infant goes from head to toe. Typically, babies' first motor milestones are lifting their heads and gaining control of their necks. Next their backs and trunks become stronger, and they can sit. Then their legs strengthen so they can stand. From there, the finer motor development extends from the trunk through the arms. Babies begin to use their arms before their hands—and their hands before their fingers.

Around the third or fourth month, life with a baby begins to settle in just a little. Parents—and grandparents, if you spend a lot of time with your grandchild—are better at reading the baby's signals. Parents may be taking steps to establish a routine. At bedtime, grandchildren this age may cry or fuss while learning to fall asleep alone. Experts agree that a little crying doesn't affect the attachment a baby feels for the caregivers or relatives. Even if a baby cries at bedtime, it's almost a sure thing he or she will be smiling the next morning.

WHAT'S NEW

The need for a good night's sleep is nothing new, but in the years since we were parents, experts have developed more detailed advice about how to achieve it. Most agree one of the essential developmental milestones is a baby learning to self-soothe. You'll probably hear the term "CIO" or "crying it out." Methods based on CIO advocate allowing a baby to cry for a certain period of time without gaining attention from parents. Most proponents recommend that parents wait until the baby is four months old to introduce this method.

This phase of family life is nothing new—babies, sooner or later, become able to sleep through the night without parental intervention. I remember my mother encouraging me with my children, promising that no seventeen-year-old has ever needed to be rocked to sleep! In fact, in 1985 a pediatrician named Richard Ferber wrote a book entitled *Solve Your Child's Sleep Problems*. The book was updated in 2006. The director emeritus of the Sleep Center at Boston Children's Hospital, Dr. Ferber has become so associated with "crying it out" that any approach using his "waiting" techniques is often referred to as "Ferberizing." Today, there are other experts, including Dr. Marc Weissbluth, Dr. William Sears, and Elizabeth Pantley, who offer their own versions of sleep advice.

The essential crying-it-out method involves "progressive waiting." Parents place the baby in bed, using a nightly routine meant to calm and comfort. Then they leave the baby. They allow the baby to cry for a specific period of time before going back into the room to comfort the baby very briefly. The parent soothes, pats, and then leaves again—and then, this time, gives the baby a little more time to cry before going back in. This sleep-training period for some babies lasts one night—for others, it doesn't seem to work. Some parents simply can't stand to stay away while the baby cries.

While your grandchild is learning to self-soothe, be sure to ask the parents questions about how you can help—especially if you will be babysitting overnight. That way, you will be following your grandbaby's parents' lead from the sidelines, and be ready to follow the bedtime routine once it's established.

And you thought you'd never have to go through toilet training again!

The fact that the topic of "infant toilet training" would even come up in a book about a baby's first year is something new to most Americans. This method involves letting a baby go diaperless. The idea is for parents to learn their baby's signs for the need to eliminate—this is sometimes called "elimination communication"—and for the baby to learn to hold back the activity until parents say it's okay. This approach is actually a long-standing custom in some other cultures, even though it's still relatively uncommon in the U.S.

An infant can urinate up to twenty times a day, so proponents of infant toilet training generally recommend beginning after the baby reaches three months of age. Many parents appreciate that diaperless toilet training produces far less waste (as in disposable diapers). But this method is easier to apply in societies that accept the idea of a baby or small child being diaperless and eliminating in public. Parents who aren't comfortable with that will have to keep their babies at home and prepare to spend much of their time watching closely.

The more traditional approach to toilet training, which is generally agreed upon by medical experts such as the American Academy of Pediatrics, the American Academy of Family Physicians, and the Mayo Clinic, is based on the concept of the child's own readiness.

Children achieve readiness at different ages, but generally not before the age of eighteen months, which is around the time they begin to gain control of their bowels and bladder. Experts do stress that consistency is important for successful toilet training. Chances are you won't be deciding which

THE MAYO CLINIC'S
LIST OF READINESS CUES

- Does your child seem interested in the potty chair or toilet or in wearing underwear?
- Can your child understand and follow basic directions?
- Does your child tell you through words, facial expressions, or posture when he or she needs to go?
- Does your child stay dry for periods of two hours or longer during the day?
- Does your child complain about wet or dirty diapers?
- Can your child pull down his or her pants and pull them up again?
- Can your child sit on and rise from a potty chair?

approach to use for toilet training—or at what age to start—so you just need to be ready to go along with what the parents decide.

Most babies are trained by sometime between twenty-four and thirty-six months. Since this book is about a baby's first year, that's all we have to say about that at this time.

I never became a master at the more traditional approach to toilet training, even though I read a lot about it and employed the recommended methods. My sons rebuffed whatever approach I tried, unless it involved a Star Wars action figure as a reward.

Keeping things clean and safe at the same time

When a baby starts spending time in more rooms of the house, there's a tendency to want to sanitize everything. Parents are more careful these days about chemicals because it is well known that harsh chemicals can affect a baby's eyes, airways, and skin. You might be able to find products without these chemicals if you look for "green" and nontoxic cleaners. Some labels may indicate that products are petroleum free, biodegradable, phosphate free, VOC free, or solvent free. You could also go the natural route and use diluted vinegar for cleaning windows or baking soda and water as a kitchen cleaner. Experts advise diluting cleaning products with water and limiting the use of antibacterial soap. When cleaning carpets, avoid spray cleaners that leave residual chemicals where your rug rat is likely to sniff them. Instead, use a steam cleaner with water and no detergent. And forgo products that promise that good-and-clean pine or lemon smell—because those scents come from added chemicals.

Child-care centers often use a solution of bleach and water—and some are required by law to do so—to disinfect surfaces, equipment, and toys. While bleach kills germs quickly and then breaks down to harmless components, the fumes are irritating and some people believe they are toxic. Your grandchild's parents may have their own opinion, so follow their lead. They might have found alternate products, or they may think some use of bleach is acceptable—but avoid using bleach or any cleaning product when babies are in the room.

When it comes to germs, common sense tells us to keep babies away from anyone who is sick. Most illness comes from exposure to someone who is already ill. Getting outside in the fresh air isn't as risky. So you can certainly venture out with your grandchild.

All about "baby-wearing"

In many societies, children traditionally have been wrapped against their mother's bodies in cloths or shawls, and that's where they spend most of their time. Some societies still carry on that custom. In other countries, the carriages and buggies that we use today became the norm. In the 1970s and 1980s, the wrapping and wearing methods that provide physical contact gained a renewed popularity. Some people believe this contact supports better development.

In the early 1980s, a sling was developed to provide modern mothers with easy "baby-wearing." Carriers now come in a wide variety of styles, and different types fit babies at different stages. If your grandchild likes to be carried that way, and his or her parents invite you to "carry on," you'll want to find one that's safe and comfortable for you. Try it—you might like it and you may discover that a baby who has trouble falling asleep will often be comforted and lulled to sleep when "worn." Also, as your grandchild gains weight, you'll find a carrier takes some stress off your arms.

Sun protection is absolutely necessary

Why is it that when you see someone in the sun wearing a hat, it's usually a grandma or a granddad? It's because we learned about the dangers of sun exposure too late. But today's parents, even if they don't always protect their own skin, take many more precautions to protect their babies' skin.

Babies are particularly susceptible to sunburn because their skin is so thin. It's now known that a single case of significant sunburn during infancy or childhood can double the risk of melanoma (the most serious kind of skin cancer) later in life. The best advice is to keep younger babies (under six months) out of the sun as much as possible, and when they are going to be exposed, to cover their skin with a hat or the hood of a stroller. You might laugh at the idea of your little one in sunglasses, but sunlight can harm a baby's eyes, too. By six months, a baby should still stay out of the sun as much as possible, and parents and grandparents can begin applying broad spectrum sunscreen.

Fortunately swimsuits and cover-ups for infants and children (adults, too) are now available in sun-protective fabric from many sources such as Athleta, Coolibar, Solartex, UV Skinz, and Parasol.

WHAT ABOUT BUGS?

As with sunscreen, you probably don't want to apply insect repellant to a child under six months of age. The other options are to keep babies indoors at dusk when mosquitoes are most active or to use mosquito netting on the stroller. Once your grandchild is six months old, insect repellent is safe to apply. Some are specifically formulated for children, and many are made with safe ingredients like citronella or soybean oil.

Modern parents are aware and wary

Many of today's parents oppose the use of chemicals and certain plastics in their baby's eating utensils and GMOs (genetically modified organisms) in their food.

BPA, which stands for bisphenol A, is an industrial chemical found in some plastic products. Many believe that it can seep into food or beverages and negatively affect brain development. Some products are labeled BPA-free. You can also read recycle codes on the bottom of containers. Code numbers 3 and 7 indicate that the item contains BPA. Code 1 means that the plastic does not contain BPA. For hot foods and liquids, glass, porcelain, or stainless steel containers are better than plastic ones.

What happens with a GMO is that DNA from another organism has been used to give the food desirable qualities. Buying foods that are certified as USDA organic can help you avoid feeding your grandchild GMOs if that's a concern for you.

There are other chemicals and substances that are particularly harmful to little ones. (Truthfully, they aren't so good for big people either, but smaller amounts affect babies more or differently than they do adults.) Those commonly mentioned include arsenic (trace amounts are found in some juices), flame retardants, fluoride (helps fight cavities, but too much isn't good and babies shouldn't use toothpaste or mouthwash until they can spit it out), formaldehyde, lead, mercury (in some fish), and pesticides. A good source of updated information is the Children's Environmental Health Center of Mount Sinai Hospital, which lists more than thirty potentially harmful substances: http://www.mountsinai.org/patient-care/service-areas/children /areas-of-care/childrens-environmental-health-center/childrens -disease-and-the-environment/environmental-toxins.

WHAT YOU CAN DO

Babies this age love:

- Singsong melodies
- Funny faces
- Making adults laugh
- "Raspberries" on the tummy or the feet (well, *some* babies love this)
- Dancing in your arms

At this age, babies want sensory stimulation—and that stimulation will support healthy development. Focus on sight, sound, and touch.

Watching a baby look at things can be fascinating. You can make an effort to surround your grandchild with stimulating toys and books. Keep in mind that babies tend to like sharp and contrasting colors, as well as black-and-white designs, more than muted colors. The best books for your grandchild at this age are the ones that have bold and simple illustrations. The story line doesn't really matter.

At this age, babies still prefer to gaze sideways rather than looking straight up at something. To encourage your grandchild to track moving objects, move a toy or other item from one side of the baby's sight line to the other. When your grandbaby starts reaching for objects, remember that young babies will be more likely to reach for an item offered from the side rather than from the front. And babies also love looking at faces—especially their own faces. Introduce your grandchild to the baby in the mirror.

You also can stimulate your grandbaby with sounds and words. At this age, continue to talk to your grandchild and, especially as the six-month mark approaches, expand your repertoire. Point out qualities of the objects in front of both of you: the blanket is soft, the light is bright. Describe their purpose: socks keep your feet warm, the spoon stirs the food. Tune in to sounds together: The dog is barking, woof, woof. Look at the truck, vroom-vroom. You can also begin asking your grandchild to respond to commands like waving bye-bye or giving Granddad a hug—but don't expect the appropriate response just yet.

Baby massage is a popular way to provide more relaxing sensory stimulation. Be sure to choose a quiet moment that is not too soon after a meal. Massage can stimulate circulation and respiration, decrease stress hormones, boost the immune system, and improve muscle development. If your grandbaby's parents have developed a massage routine, follow their lead. Experts suggest that you keep your hands on the baby at all times and maintain eye contact. Use a gentle touch and soft baby lotion—and be sure to warm it first by rubbing it in your hands. Experiment with different massage strokes to see what your grandbaby likes best.

Strike a balance between stimulation and alone time

Of course, that doesn't mean *alone* alone. Create times when you can monitor the baby without interfering. You don't want your grandchild to develop a need for constant entertainment. If you pause in your interaction, your grandbaby has a chance to lead the way and decide how to play. You may think a ball is for rolling, but a baby may prefer to poke or pat it. Don't be afraid to give your grandchild the chance to stare into space or inspect a fiber of the rug or chew on a toe. It's all entertaining to a baby. And watching can be fun for you. With a child this young, it may not last long—maybe just a few minutes—but let it happen.

KEEPING IN TOUCH LONG DISTANCE

If you don't live close enough to your grandchild and his or her parents to see them frequently, you may want to take advantage of technology to still enjoy "visits." Ask your son or daughter and their partner about Skype or FaceTime. Online journals and scrapbooks such as Lifecake, Tinybeans, Moment Garden, Kidmondo, and Tweekaboo are popular and offer various features, including giving parents a format and platform for uploading photos and videos with comments to share privately with family and friends.

Is knowledge power?

With access to so much new and developing information about healthy practices, you may run across advice or recommendations that conflict with what your daughter or son and their partner are doing. Remind yourself that several different opinions or approaches may be valid, especially when studies and techniques are still developing. Then realistically assess how receptive the parents might be to suggestions. Some new parents are happy to hear another opinion. Others will take any attempt to start the conversation as a threat or insult. Sometimes the best suggestion is offered as a question.

The best part of learning about babies and children is that you won't be caught off guard. You'll have a context for the new, unexpected, curious, or wonderful things that are bound to occur.

All of That

Who are you, baby?
More than soft skin
and urgent emotion,
spending all that time
just being alive.
Are you in a hurry, baby—
to move and roll,
clutch and kick?
Or is lying there just right,
watching and listening to
all that surrounds you?
Is your Self taking shape,
made of particles
as old as time,
yet so brand new?
May you become
strong enough to be sturdy,
soft enough to be sweet,
clear enough to be honest,
bright enough to understand.
Who are you, baby,
right at this moment,
this very instant?
You are all of that.
And more.

CHAPTER 5
Action (6–12 Months)

WHAT'S STILL TRUE

A personality emerges

During this period, babies become much more interactive. They add sounds to their babbling vocabularies and fine-tune their motor skills. As they approach that first birthday, they will increasingly engage you in "conversations," during which you mimic the sound the baby makes and the baby attempts to mimic you. This is when babies learn their names. They like games. They drop something (anything!) off their high chair so you can have fun retrieving it. They also begin to be suspicious about unfamiliar people. If you haven't seen your grandchild in a while, don't be offended if he or she doesn't immediately recognize you. He or she might look at mommy or daddy as if to say, "Is this person okay?" Just give your grandbaby a little time to get reacquainted. Not all babies are equally extroverted—some are more reserved or contemplative. You will begin to see signs of a personality emerge.

According to many child development experts, babies are fascinated with other children from a very early age—but they probably see that child as an interesting object that moves and makes sounds without understanding the concept of "baby" or "playmate." For example, until around age two, if another child grabs your grandchild's toy, she or he will probably not care at all because it's just so interesting to watch the child with the toy. Even after age two, children who often played side by side with other children (commonly called "parallel play") at a young age tend to be more tolerant.

Teeth emerge, too

Babies get their first teeth at different times, but generally at least one tooth pops up by age one. Most babies sprout teeth a little earlier, around six or seven months. Typically, babies have eight teeth by the end of their twelfth month and add eight more by the time they are two years old. The signs of teething haven't changed—irritability because of painful gums, some extra drooling, and the desire to put everything in his or her mouth. Our mothers told us that teething also causes fevers and diarrhea, but chances are our daughters or daughter-in-laws have learned that isn't true. There is also another big reason babies drool around the age of four or five months: Their salivary glands are getting ready to digest solid food.

We're eager to see our babies crawl

With the current practice of back sleeping, some babies are crawling later than they used to—and some may miss that milestone altogether. They haven't necessarily developed the upper body strength that tummy-sleeping babies did. Even when our children were babies, researchers understood that crawling is important for more than just developing trunk and shoulder muscles. All sorts of cognitive functions are developed and strengthened during the crawling stage, including hand-eye coordination, binocular vision (looking at something far away and then close), and cross-lateral movement that stimulates communication between left and right sides of the brain (which is important for reading). It's said that crawling strengthens the tongue muscles that help with speech.

There is even a theory that lack of crawling is related to learning disabilities, possibly attention deficit hyperactivity disorder (ADHD). Crawling helps strengthen the reflex known as "symmetric tonic neck reflex" (STNR). An immature STNR can lead to difficulties that contribute to a disability, such as clumsiness or slumping when sitting at a desk.

If that inspires you to encourage your grandbaby to crawl, there are a few things you can do. When your grandchild is not sleeping, encourage tummy time. Play games that put objects and toys slightly out of reach, or move them out of reach as you play. Get down on your own hands and knees and show baby how much fun it is to crawl.

WHAT'S NEW

Advice about teething remedies has changed

What is the current advice on helping a baby when he or she is teething? Not whiskey rubbed on the gums. And no, not gel. Medical experts recommend *against* using any teething relief product that contains the chemical benzocaine, which most teething gels do. In 2010, the FDA also stepped in to recall a homeopathic teething tablet containing belladonna, which can be toxic to the nervous system. Since then, the manufacturers state they have reformulated their products to contain miniscule amounts of belladonna—and it has not been recalled since then. Whether or not that's reassurance enough is a personal decision.

Another teething pain "remedy" that has raised serious alarms is the amber necklace. This is an example of the value of turning to science rather than popular culture to make good decisions. Adopters of the amber necklace claim amber contains an analgesic substance called succinic acid that is released by the beads in response to the warmth of the child's body and absorbed through the skin. But there is no scientific evidence to suggest that the acid is released at human body temperature—or that it has an analgesic effect. More importantly, these necklaces pose choking and strangulation hazards. Many countries where these necklaces are sold and worn are taking steps. For example, in Canada, the federal department of public health issued a safety warning about the risks, and in France and Switzerland, the sale of amber necklaces in pharmacies has been banned.

For safe pain relief, experts are now recommending only acetaminophen (like Tylenol) and ibuprofen (like Advil). There are also old-fashioned remedies such as massaging the baby's gums or freezing a bagel, a banana, or a washcloth and letting the baby gnaw on that. Hopefully, the new parents instruct you according to their chosen method.

Introducing your grandbaby to the joy of eating

The introduction of solid foods is a significant step because eating habits and taste preferences begin to be established. The baby's parents probably will have strong opinions on the topic, based either on their physician's advice or their friends' anecdotes or both.

Many of today's parents are intent upon eliminating chemicals in their baby's food. Some are making their own food. In fact, sales of commercial baby food have declined steadily since 2005. Other parents only purchase store-bought food that is organically certified. These organic products are more widely available than they were even a decade ago because baby-food makers have responded to the changing market.

Parents who prefer to make baby food from scratch may use food mills, stick blenders, or even the gadgets that steam and purée at once. When I bought baby food for my children, the choices were limited—chicken, turkey, beans, peas, carrots, squash—and smelled pretty unappetizing. These days, the flavors vary greatly and include ingredients like kale, pomegranate, cumin, thyme, and quinoa. Will today's babies grow up with more sophisticated palates? We'll see.

When my children began eating finger foods, we never left home without a baggie of Cheerios in case an outing started to go downhill. Today's moms and dads have more options. There are organic varieties of edible "puffs" that are mostly air with

a little flavoring, and serve the same purpose. I've also seen some conversations online asking where zwieback (that hard biscuit babies used to love to gnaw on) has gone. Today's substitutes for the zwieback biscuits many of us remember include "biter biscuits," but some babies can choke when the biscuits are chewed down to a small size. Proceed carefully. Crackers that get mushy in the mouth are a safer finger food—and *might* allow adults to finish a meal in a restaurant.

Some other things you'll want to keep in mind as your grandbaby begins to eat solid foods include:

CHOKING: Babies and small children are particularly vulnerable to choking because their narrow airways are easily obstructed. They don't become really good at chewing until age two or three. Until that time, the foods considered most likely to cause choking are raw vegetables like celery and carrots, whole peas that are not smashed or puréed, firm fruits like apples and unripe pears, fruits with seeds, grapes, raisins, popcorn, potato chips, nuts, hard candy, meat, and hot dogs. Marshmallows, globs of peanut butter, and chewing gum are also almost impossible for new eaters to manage. To play it safe, avoid these foods and always supervise mealtimes, no matter what your grandchild is eating.

BABY-LED WEANING: Most of us started our own children on solid foods by introducing rice cereal at an early age. Baby-led weaning is an alternative to feeding mush or puréed food with a spoon and involves small pieces the baby can pick up in his or her fingers, developing the pincer grasp along with a taste for real food. Parents who adopt this approach often feed the baby the same menu the rest of the family is eating (of course, being sure to avoid the foods that pose a choking hazard). If the parents are following the guideline of breastfeeding until the baby is six months old, the weaning can begin at this time.

Be aware of potential allergens

Allergies are an increasingly common concern for today's parents. Allergic reactions are actually responses from the immune system, which recognizes a "threat" and attacks it. Allergies that affect the respiratory system cause coughing, sneezing, and runny noses. Those that affect the intestinal tract result in vomiting and diarrhea (usually these symptoms come from food allergies). And those that affect the skin cause hives, rashes, and uncomfortable itching.

Experts used to think that a baby's immune system wasn't capable of launching such an attack—and that babies could not have allergic reactions—but that opinion has changed. Reactions to common allergens such as dust, mold, pet dander, or food can appear early in life. Seasonal allergies tend to occur after the baby has had at last one season to develop the allergy.

WHAT FOODS CAUSE ALLERGIES?

Just a short list of foods tends to be the prime suspects in causing 90 percent of food allergies. This list includes cow's milk, egg whites, nuts, fish and shellfish, wheat, soy, cocoa, citrus fruits, berries, and sesame seeds.

To reduce the chances of a child being allergic to foods, today's parents are advised to have the baby breastfeed exclusively until four to six months of age and then introduce new foods slowly, waiting several days after a new food is introduced to see how that food is tolerated. If you follow the parents' menu and instructions, you can avoid unintentionally causing a first allergic reaction!

As for introducing foods on that "most allergic" list, the thinking of medical experts has changed. You've probably heard a lot about peanut allergies, which can be serious and even life threatening. Although actual peanuts are avoided because they pose a choking hazard for children under age three, many peanut ingredients are included in other foods. As recently as the year 2000, doctors were recommending that the introduction of peanut products and other foods suspected of causing allergies should be delayed until after the age of three. As a result, many parents thought that avoiding foods such as those with peanut ingredients decreased the chance of developing an allergy to that food. But new research suggests, and the American Academy of Allergy, Asthma & Immunology recommends, that exposing a child to those foods (in a non-choking form such as peanut puffs) between the ages of four and eleven months may actually reduce the likelihood of that child having an allergy.

Likewise, experts now believe that exposure to other allergens, such as pet dander, may actually protect a child from developing an allergy to them. In other words, they suggest children who live with pets are less likely to develop an allergy to pet dander. As with all research, additional studies may confirm or contradict this new approach, so parents need to stay informed.

If you are concerned that your grandchild might have a particular allergy, ask your daughter or son and their partner to get detailed advice from their pediatrician. If other members of the family suffer from allergies, the pediatrician may recommend allergy screenings. Allergies tend to run in families, so if either of the parents or their relatives have allergies, your grandbaby may develop some, too. If one parent has allergies, a child's chance of being allergic is about 30 percent; if both parents have allergies, the risk is raised to 60 percent. For children whose parents have no allergies, the risk is only about 15 percent.

Once a child is known to have an allergy to a substance such as peanuts, caution is advised. Air travel is particularly concerning for parents of children and babies with nut allergies. There is no law prohibiting peanuts from being served on planes. Some flight crews and airlines will agree to establish a peanut-free zone—several rows in front of and behind the person with the allergy—if they receive a call in advance, or allow a parent to board early and wipe down the surrounding area.

Too bad they're not allergic to electronic devices

Most homes today offer babies a variety of tempting screens—TVs, computers, tablets, and phones. But many medical experts are concerned about letting children spend time with these devices. Your grandchild's brain is developing so quickly during these early months, and babies learn best from interactions with people, not screens. For many years, the American Academy of Pediatrics (AAP) has recommended that television and other entertainment media should be avoided for children under the age of two. Because digital devices are so much a part of our culture, the AAP is continually reviewing the scientific research, releasing its findings, and making appropriate recommendations.

ADDITIONAL RESEARCH ON YOUNG CHILDREN AND TV

PBS (Public Broadcasting System) and other groups also study the topic of how television affects children. Research published in *Behavioral Science* found that in homes where the TV is on all or most of the time—even just in the background—children were less likely to be able to read and had shorter attention spans.

Another concern about screen-watching is that it takes the place of physical activity and independent play. Some people believe that children are too young to understand the educational games and technologies available, and that an early introduction to those devices might lead to an unhealthy habit or dependence.

Be aware that even very young children gravitate toward screens. My son and daughter-in-law agreed that their baby had better things to do than watch screens and kept their TV off and their devices out of reach. But my grandson, well before he was a year old, was eager to get his hands on their iPhones and had learned to press the Siri button to hear her voice.

An early way to communicate: baby sign language

Since the early 2000s, baby sign language has gained popularity because it enables babies to communicate before they learn to speak. Parents who favor baby sign language believe it eases frustration and may lead to higher IQ scores. But some experts caution parents who use baby sign language not to neglect verbal skills at the same time.

Concerns over autism are on the rise

Parents are much more concerned about autism than we were twenty or thirty years ago. Is the incidence of autism increasing? Are methods of diagnosis that much better? Or has autism merely caught the attention of the media?

In early 2014, the CDC announced that autism cases in the U.S. had risen 30 percent in two years—from one in eighty-eight children to one in sixty-eight children. But health officials believe that the statistics show an increase because of changes in the practice of assessment and diagnosis. The good news is that with early intervention and treatment, many autistic children lead happy and meaningful lives.

You may have cause for concern if a child nearing the age of one cannot or does not:

- make eye contact
- smile when smiled at
- follow objects visually
- do "back-and-forth gestures" such as pointing, showing, reaching, or waving "bye-bye"
- initiate or respond to cuddling
- follow the gesture when you point something out
- have warm smiles or big playful expressions

Another warning sign is when a child regresses or can no longer perform a skill mastered earlier. It would be a difficult conversation to have, but if you believe your grandchild is exhibiting signs of autism, you should certainly speak up.

In recent years, a debate over whether there might be a connection between autism and immunizations has received a fair amount of media attention. But in early 2015, Autism Speaks, the U.S.'s largest autism advocacy group, issued a statement negating any link between autism and immunizations. The spokesperson for the group said, "Vaccines do not cause autism. We urge that all children be fully vaccinated."

WHAT YOU CAN DO

The baby begins to play back

There's a big difference between playing peek-a-boo with a baby who is too young to pull the cloth off your head and playing with a baby who pulls the cloth off your head and then squeals with happiness. I won't predict when it will happen—but it will, and you'll feel a surge of joy. With my grandbaby, it seemed to coincide with crawling, as if having choices about where he could go made him more proactive in his play.

Bounce the baby on your knees to the beat of any old song. Knock over a tower of soft blocks together. Clap to music. Play copycat. If you don't mind being a little silly, there's no limit to opportunities for play. Laughing together benefits everyone. It's an excellent way to bond, it's a stress reliever, and it can actually boost your immune system—and your grandbaby's.

The more you talk to your grandchild, the more he or she learns about communication, including sound, tone of voice, facial expressions, and body language. Studies have shown that a conversation—rather than a monologue—has a greater

BE SPONTANEOUS

One of our favorite games came about spontaneously during the Christmas holidays. We named it "Swipe the Bow off Papa's Nose." I started by pressing the sticky-backed bow from a gift on my very tolerant husband's nose. Our then-eleven-month-old grandchild grabbed it off, and we all laughed. Pretty soon the baby was handing the bow back to his granddad so they could play the game over and over.

impact on language skills. In other words, asking questions and letting the baby "answer" is a good idea.

A little tickling goes a long way

Believe it or not, people disagree about tickling babies. Some feel that it's a great way to connect with a baby and laugh together. Others feel that it's taking advantage of your size and strength—you have all the power. There's even one old wives' tale that warns tickling causes stuttering. (Not true. Stuttering, a fluency problem, usually appears between two and four years of age. It's more common in boys than in girls, and it tends to run in families.)

The best advice about tickling seems to be: Don't overdo it. Babies can't say "stop" and even small children get laughing so hard, they can't say "stop"—and if it goes on too long (or if the baby never likes it in the first place) it's not fun. Instead, pretend to tickle without touching the baby's sides. Pretend to munch on the baby's toes or fingers. Or give the baby the upper hand—for example, pretend the baby has you down on the floor, tickling you, and you can't get up.

Start a lifelong love of reading

If you want to read with a baby of this age, go into it with an open mind. The baby is as likely to chew on the book as to let you read it. At first, babies will manipulate the book in their hands but won't turn the pages. They may get tired of the book before you get to the end.

A suggestion from experts is that you try to engage the baby with the images in the book—pointing at pictures, repeating the names of those objects in a varying pitch and tone—but don't worry if the story gets lost. Eventually, the baby will treat the book like a book, and the story like a story—but that won't happen right away.

In addition to Too Small to Fail, mentioned earlier in the book, another organization with the mission of encouraging parents (and grandparents!) to read to their children is Read Aloud 15 Minutes (http://www.readaloud.org). This not-for-profit group cites research showing reading aloud is the most important thing you can do to help prepare a child for reading and learning, but reports that, unfortunately, only 40 percent of young children in the U.S. are read to each day. Read Aloud is on a mission to get parents to read to their child for at least fifteen minutes a day, every day. When you are with your grandchild, you can make that fifteen minutes of reading happen—or even better, add an extra fifteen minutes on top of what the parents are doing. Find a nice, quiet time—maybe right before nap or bedtime—and settle in together with a good book.

Your little one will develop his or her own favorite bedtime books, but many children enjoy *Goodnight Moon*; *Goodnight, Goodnight Construction Site*; *The Going to Bed Book*; *The Goodnight Train*; and *Time for Bed*. These and other bedtime books make excellent gifts for parents, but are also a good staple for grandparents' homes for when your grandchild comes to visit.

Grandparents as babysitters

The term "babysitting" was coined in the late 1930s when young families started moving out of their traditional neighborhoods where the extended family members all took part in raising a baby. The term literally meant "sit" with the baby while the parents were elsewhere.

If you are willing and able to "sit" with your grandchild on occasion, don't be too proud to ask the parents for specific instructions. There's nothing quite like hearing a frenzied baby cry while you struggle to put the gizmo on the whatchamacallit and get a bottle ready for the first time in decades.

Grandparents are often the primary caregivers for a child outside of his or her parents. The U.S. Census Bureau studied the topic of grandparents caring for their grandchildren in 2012 and found that 2.7 million grandparents were actually raising their grandchildren. Statistics also show that grandparents are the primary source of child care for 30 percent of women who work.

Another study, conducted in 2008 by Johns Hopkins University, found that grandparents are likely to be the very best caregivers in the parents' absence. The research showed that a baby's risk of injury was cut by approximately half if the grandmother took care of the child rather than a day care center, another relative, or another unrelated mother. It is clear that grandparents feel especially protective. That doesn't surprise you, does it?

As grandparents, we may feel a temptation to try to repeat everything we did with our own children. Some of that may still work, but remember to adapt your style to the passage of time, if necessary. If you are in the physical condition to roll around on the floor and give piggyback rides, then go ahead and enjoy it. But there are many ways to be a grandparent. Acknowledge your physical quirks or limitations so you don't put the baby or yourself at risk. And plan ahead so that you can provide the safest environment for your grandbaby.

Carry the baby up and down stairs only if you are strong and sure-footed. Walk back and forth endlessly with a nearly sleeping baby only if you have the stamina. Otherwise, rocking a baby to sleep is easier to sustain. Avoid twisting knees and straining backs. Your grandchild's parents should help develop systems that work comfortably for you, since they want you to be confident and safe around the baby. Physical therapists advise that everyone, when picking up the child, bend at the knees, not hips. Widen your legs to get a broad base of support. Hold the child close to you and your center of gravity. Keep your shoulders back and avoid slouching under the added weight.

Baby-proof the house

Basic baby-proofing is especially important if your grandchild spends time in your home. Here's a partial checklist of some important safeguards:

- Cover sharp edges of furniture with molded plastic pieces made for this purpose.
- Secure sliding doors.
- Put window shade cords and lamp cords out of reach.
- Cover electrical outlets.
- Secure or lock cabinet doors.
- Remove anything fragile or heavy from where the baby might reach. For example, a camera on a table with a strap hanging down is an invitation for the baby to pull it down on top of him or her.
- Inspect surfaces and remove any small objects that pose a choking risk, especially batteries, pet treats and toys, coins, buttons, paper clips, or small pieces of food or candy. Purses are wonderlands of small, enticing, and dangerous objects. Keep them in the closet.
- Keep plastic bags away from the baby.
- Be especially careful with latex balloons—they can be inhaled and then block the child's airway. Don't let babies play with balloons. If they pop, throw the pieces away immediately.
- Point knives and forks with the sharp parts facing down in the dishwasher's utensil basket. Keep the dishwasher door closed and locked.

Magnets are a particularly devastating hazard. If a baby or young child swallows two magnets and they are attracted to each other inside the child's digestive tract, it may be impossible for the magnets to pass through the tract. If they are in separate loops of the intestines and are attracted to each other, they can cause the intestines to become perforated. Toys with magnets don't belong within reach of children under the age of three.

Continue to check areas as the baby moves from room to room, in case something has fallen on the floor or been moved around. As the baby gets older and begins to climb on things, you will need a whole new level of security—for example, checking for windows with screens that can be pushed out.

THEY LOOK LIKE CANDY— BUT THEY'RE NOT!

On the list of new hazards are the dishwasher soap packets that look like bright, juicy candy—just what a baby can't resist. If you use them, keep them out of reach. Of course, liquid and powdered detergents are equally hazardous. Bath oils or cosmetics containing oil are also potentially harmful. When swallowed, they can cause asphyxiation and even irreversible lung damage.

To know you is to love you

Now that we've taken care of safety, let's get back to joy. There is no guarantee that the baby who now snuggles into your neck or laughs when you make silly faces will always consider you special. During the first months of life, babies typically just want their needs met and do not differentiate among the adults who take care of them. But over time, they develop their favorites— mom and dad, of course—so wouldn't it be great if you can be a favorite, too? However often you see your grandbaby and regardless of the time you are able to spend, the genuine love you feel and show has rewards because you are helping this baby feel secure and loved.

Traditions and transitions

In many families, grandparents hold the key to history and traditions. It's the family getting together on the Fourth of July, or putting out the cookies for Santa on the same plate every Christmas Eve, or whatever it is you established as a custom for your family while your children were young. Some of those patterns may even have been handed down from your own parents. I've been surprised that my typically not-so-sentimental sons remember certain moments and certain rituals and want to repeat them. So I have learned not to dismiss or dismantle traditions too quickly when they become less convenient.

But along with traditions come transitions. Perhaps in the early years of your son's or daughter's marriage, you were able to keep some of those customs intact, or adapted them as necessary to the customs of your in-laws. With a baby, your daughter or son and their partner may want to start new traditions of their own. Don't be surprised if they want to spend a holiday in their home for the first time. As grandparents, we need to strike that balance and decide what's really important to keep our family close and connected.

The traits and qualities of effective grandparents

What does it mean to be an effective grandparent, one that has a positive and lasting—and maybe even indispensable— influence on a young person's life? The Foundation for Grandparenting conducted a survey to find out if people thought grandparents were an indispensable part of their families. You'll be happy to know that 77 percent of those surveyed said yes. The study also concluded that a grandparent's degree of effectiveness wasn't determined by age or gender or ethnic origin but rather tended to come from certain personal traits. Those that emerged as being important were:

- Altruism—an attitude toward life that includes wanting to make things better for other people
- Certain temperaments or personalities that behave a certain way—being patient, willing to listen and understand, being responsive
- Availability—making an effort to spend time with a grandchild
- Readiness—feeling that the time is right to take on the grandparenting role (It was noted that the readiness factor comes into play especially for grandfathers who tend to mellow somewhat as they age and now take special pleasure in activities they didn't appreciate earlier in their lives.)
- Experience and life philosophy—viewing family relationships as important, perhaps because their own grandparents were important to them
- Positive, proactive involvement with the grandchild's parents and other family members based on the desire to be a source of strength and support.

And my favorite: vitality—exuberance, energy, the capacity for survival or the continuation of a purposeful and meaningful existence. This vitality can be physical, intellectual, spiritual, or emotional. It is a sense that life is worth living, that life is an adventure, that something new and worthwhile might be just around the corner. And what a grandparent gives in this regard, he or she surely receives in return. As people get older, they sometimes lose vitality. A grandchild is one more reason to embrace life for its new possibilities.

My Biggest Fan

You think I'm hilarious.
I think you already have
a good sense of humor
for someone so young.
I bang a spoon
and you bang back.
Then we both laugh.
I shake my head
and you shake yours.
Then we both laugh.
I make the stuffed pig oink
And you squeal.
I'm a comedian.
And you're my biggest fan.

CHAPTER 6
Advice (For a Lifetime)

Be here now

You might remember that in the early 1970s, psychologist Richard Alpert transformed himself into a yogi master and changed his name to Baba Ram Dass. He wrote the book *Be Here Now* to help people incorporate Hindu philosophy, yoga, and meditation into their spiritual journeys. You will probably see that your grandbaby already knows everything about "being here now."

You unveil a new toy, and the baby is fascinated with the wrapper. The urge is to pull it away and bring attention to the toy—but to "be here now," you will let the baby explore it. When you step outside together, the baby may be amazed by the change in environment—the sunshine, the breeze, the leaves on the trees waving and fluttering, the sound of birds chirping. To "be here now," you can pause and take it all in together.

Many cultures, religions, philosophies, and forms of spirituality have their own principles of living in the moment, being open to experience. With a baby in mind, these sayings are particularly relevant reminders of how we, as grandparents, can watch, wonder, and learn with our little ones.

Observations from great thinkers

"We don't receive wisdom; we must discover it for ourselves after a journey that no one can take for us or spare us."

—MARCEL PROUST

"Nothing important comes with instructions."

—JAMES RICHARDSON

"This very moment is the perfect teacher, and lucky for us, it's with us wherever we are."

—PEMA CHODRON

"Learning takes place only in a mind that is innocent and vulnerable."

—KRISHNAMURTI

"Stay close to any sounds that make you glad you are alive."

—HAFEZ

"Men cannot see their reflections in running water, but only in still water."

—CHUANG-TZU

"In order to see birds, it is important to become part of the silence."

—ROBERT LYND

"Attention is the rarest and purest form of generosity."

—SIMONE WEIL

"Truly, I say to you, unless you turn and become like children, you will never enter the kingdom of heaven. Whoever humbles himself like this child is the greatest in the kingdom of heaven."

—MATTHEW 18:3-4

"A child's world is fresh and new and beautiful, full of wonder and excitement. It is our misfortune that, for most of us, that clear-eyed vision, that true instinct for what is beautiful and awe-inspiring, is dimmed and even lost before we reach adulthood. If I had influence with the good fairy who is supposed to preside over the christening of all children, I should ask that her gift to each child in the world be a sense of wonder so indestructible that it would last throughout life."

—RACHEL CARSON

Real wisdom from real grandparents

"After a few months of going giddy about toys—big, bright plastic things that claimed to turn your baby into a genius—I learned to hold back. In the first place, I was being presumptuous about how much space my daughter and her husband wanted to devote to bright plastic things—and secondly, I remembered that babies often love the simplest things best. Less can be more."

—CELESTE, *grandmother of one*

"When I stopped to think about how many changes had happened in that first year, how we'd all managed to adjust, and how this little person had gotten off to a good start, I felt it was a real accomplishment."

—BILL, *grandfather of one*

"I think when you are the mother of the baby's father, you have to be a little more careful about what you say and how you say it. At first, I only felt comfortable telling my son things 'on the side' but I made myself get over that. If it was something I really want to say—or email—regarding the baby, I made sure to say it to both of them at once or not say it at all. Don't make the mistake of thinking your connection to your son is stronger than his connection to his wife."

—SUSAN, *grandmother of five*

"Do you love your son? Then love his wife!"

—JACKIE, *grandmother of seven*

"Is it tough to manage—this relationship where you are not in charge? Where you sometimes disagree but are afraid if you do that relations will become strained? It's not always easy, but you just keep doing it and you keep getting better at it."

—ALEX, *grandfather of three*

"Our new baby was a wonderful bond between members of our family. We were all busy with our own lives. But for the baby's first year, every holiday and every special occasion was about that baby. It was fun for all of us."

—PATTI, *grandmother of one*

"I made sure to include the baby's granddad and uncles and aunts when we were together. They might not have dived right into a relationship like I did, but I didn't want to be the one monopolizing her. If they didn't know how to play, I'd include them in the games."

—LENA, *grandmother of two*

"As grandparents, you find your favorite things. My wife's favorite thing to do with the baby was read books. Mine was going to the park. And very early on—by the age of about two—our grandson was the one who instigated the favorite things with each of us. And that lasted for years. I'd walk in the door and he'd come running up to me and say, 'Grandpa, can we go to the park now?'"

—LAMONT, *grandfather of four*

CONCLUSION

Your grandchild is a blank tablet on which will be written each experience that begins to form his or her life. There will be accomplishments and disappointments. Kudos and criticism. Ambition and self-doubt. Opportunities and obstacles.

You can be a force for good in this child's life, helping him or her become more confident and resilient. You can make sure your grandchild knows, without a shred or a pinprick or a speckle or a freckle of a doubt, that you are one (more) person who loves him or her completely.

And this can be one of the most satisfying relationships of your life. Having a grandchild turns on the lights where you might have dimmed the bulbs to save mental electricity. Being a grandparent changes the priorities. Upsets the schedule. Reorganizes the refrigerator. It adds a new dimension to your life, just when you were ready to cut corners, and it inspires you to be more energetic, more attentive, more compassionate, smarter, stronger, wittier, sillier, softer, and more intentional.

As a grandparent, your heart will expand with each new milestone. This is a chance for awe and wonder—and your own new growth. Don't just make it good. Make it grand!

ACKNOWLEDGMENTS

Any book is a labor of love, especially this one because it coincided with the newest love of my life, my first grandchild.

My first expression of gratitude goes to my friends who ventured into grandparenting before I did and who shared their most honest insights with me. And to all the strangers who were willing to strike up a conversation and answer my questions just because I'd noticed they were grandparents.

I thank my husband and sons, to whom this book is dedicated, because they have taught me so much about parents and children through the years. Brooke-Sidney Harbour provided many insights into new parenting methods and philosophies. She and my son Raleigh, who is one of the most devoted daddies I know, are on the front lines of my grandchild's life, and they do an amazing job.

I'm grateful to Hillary Rodham Clinton, who cherishes her role as a grandmother as strongly as any of us does and who wants a safe and bright future for our grandchildren, as we all do.

My agent, Scott Mendel of Mendel Media, was knowledgeable and patient and always had good advice. Scott's assistant, Elizabeth Dabbelt, the first person to suggest edits, contributed, too. I wouldn't have found the folks at Mendel Media without an introduction by Ray Strobel, whose experience as an author and publisher led me in the right direction.

Along the way, I was lucky to draw from the wisdom of Michael Seabaugh and Linda Renzi, each a counselor who reinforced and added dimension to my belief that grandparenting is one of life's greatest opportunities. Patti Keefe, a grandmother and R.N., gave the book an early and thorough review. Karen Storr worked with me on adapting my website Intelligent Women Dialogue (http://www.iwdialogue.com) so it can hold grandparent information, too.

I am grateful to my sister, Karen Acton Truettner, who's been a role model throughout life as well as my cheerleader—and who never hesitates to be honest. My niece Carrie Secrist Beach added creative insights, just at the right times.

I can't say enough about the team at BenBella Books. From the moment I learned that their philosophy is to work in partnership with their authors, they have been true to their word. Special gratitude goes to my excellent editor, Vy Tran, and the talented people added to our team (Jenny Bridges, Kim Broderick, Connie Gabbert). And I would like to thank everyone else at BenBella, including Glenn Yeffeth, Adrienne Lang, Sarah Dombrowsky, Alicia Kania, Jessika Rieck, and Heather Butterfield, who made this book happen. Thank you!

ABOUT THE AUTHOR

Cheryl Acton Harbour has researched and written about topics ranging from nuclear energy, education, health, learning disabilities, supply chain management, and women's leadership as a journalist and corporate communications specialist, but never with more enthusiasm than on the topic of grandparenting. Cheryl is the founder of Intelligent Women Dialogue (http://www.iwdialogue.com), an interactive forum. She is the mother of three sons and grandmother of one (so far) and lives in the Chicago area.